World of Dance

Modern
Dance

SECOND EDITION

World of Dance

African Dance, Second Edition

Asian Dance, Second Edition

Ballet, Second Edition

European Dance:
Ireland, Poland, Spain, and Greece, Second Edition

Latin and Caribbean Dance

Middle Eastern Dance, Second Edition

Modern Dance, Second Edition

Popular Dance: From Ballroom to Hip-Hop

World of Dance

Modern Dance

SECOND EDITION

Janet Anderson

**Consulting editor:
Elizabeth A. Hanley,
Associate Professor
Emerita of Kinesiology,
Penn State University**

**Foreword by
Jacques D'Amboise,
Founder of the National
Dance Institute**

CHELSEA HOUSE
PUBLISHERS

An imprint of Infobase Publishing

Chelsea House
An imprint of Infobase Publishing
132 West 31st Street
New York NY 10001

Library of Congress Cataloging-in-Publication Data
Anderson, Janet, 1952–
  Modern dance / by Janet Anderson. — 2nd ed.
    p. cm. — (World of dance)
  Includes bibliographical references and index.
  ISBN 978-1-60413-483-4 (hardcover)
  1. Modern dance—Juvenile literature. 2. Modern dance—History—Juvenile literature. I. Title. II. Series.
  GV1783.A55 2010
  792.8—dc22   2009033613

Chelsea House books are available at special discounts when purchased in bulk quantities for businesses, associations, institutions, or sales promotions. Please call our Special Sales Department in New York at (212) 967-8800 or (800) 322-8755.

You can find Chelsea House on the World Wide Web at
http://www.chelseahouse.com

Text design by Kerry Casey
Cover design by Alicia Post
Composition by EJB Publishing Services
Cover printed by Yurchak Printing, Landisville, Pa.
Book printed and bound by Yurchak Printing, Landisville, Pa.
Printed in the United States of America

This book is printed on acid-free paper.

All links and Web addresses were checked and verified to be correct at the time of publication. Because of the dynamic nature of the Web, some addresses and links may have changed since publication and may no longer be valid.

CONTENTS

Introduction   6
by Consulting Editor Elizabeth A. Hanley,
Associate Professor Emerita of Kinesiology,
Pennsylvania State University

Foreword   8
by Jacques D'Amboise,
Founder of the National Dance Institute

1   The Precursors   13

2   Denishawn   27

3   The Founding Modern-Dance Generation   39

4   The Reformers and Post-Modern Dance   51

5   Fusion   68

6   Choosing a Modern Dance Class   85

Chronology   93

Notes   96

Glossary   99

Bibliography   102

Further Resources   105

Picture Credits   111

Index   112

About the Author and Consulting Editor   117

INTRODUCTION

The world of dance is yours to enjoy! Dance has existed from time immemorial. It has been an integral part of celebrations and rituals, a means of communication with gods and among humans, and a basic source of enjoyment and beauty.

Dance is a fundamental element of human behavior and has evolved over the years from primitive movement of the earliest civilizations to traditional ethnic or folk styles, to the classical ballet and modern dance genres popular today. The term *dance* is broad and, therefore, not limited to the genres noted above. In the twenty-first century, dance includes ballroom, jazz, tap, aerobics, and a myriad of other movement activities. The joy derived from participating in dance of any genre and the physical activity required provide the opportunity for the pursuit of a healthy lifestyle in today's world.

The richness of cultural traditions observed in the ethnic, or folk, dance genre offers the participant, as well as the spectator, insight into the customs, geography, dress, and religious nature of a particular people. Originally passed on from one generation to the next, many ethnic, or folk, dances continue to evolve as our civilization and society change. From these quaint beginnings of traditional dance, a new genre emerged as a way to appeal to the upper level of society: ballet. This new form of dance rose quickly in popularity and remains so today. The genre of ethnic, or folk, dance continues to be an important part of ethnic communities throughout the United States, particularly in large cities.

When the era of modern dance emerged as a contrast and a challenge to the rigorously structured world of ballet, it was not readily accepted as an art form. Modern dance was interested in the communication of emotional experiences—through basic movement, as well as uninhibited movement—not through the academic tradition of ballet masters. Modern dance, however, found its aficionados and is a popular art form today.

No dance form is permanent, definitive, or ultimate. Changes occur, but the basic element of dance endures. Dance is for all people. One need only recall that dance needs neither common race nor common language for communication; it has been, and remains, a universal means of communication.

The WORLD OF DANCE series provides a starting point for readers interested in learning about ethnic, or folk, dances of world cultures, as well as the art forms of ballet and modern dance. This series features an overview of the development of these dance genres, from a historical perspective to a practical one. Highlighting specific cultures, their dance steps and movements, and their customs and traditions underscores the importance of these fundamental elements for the reader. Ballet and modern dance—more recent artistic dance genres—are explored in detail as well, giving the reader a comprehensive knowledge of the past, present, and potential future of each dance form.

The one fact that each reader should remember is that dance has always been, and always will be, a form of communication. This is its legacy to the world.

**

In this volume, Janet Anderson will examine the fascinating journey and development of modern dance—a relatively young art form that began at the turn of the twentieth century. Pioneers such as Loie Fuller, Isadora Duncan, and Ruth St. Denis would break from dance traditions such as ballet, but would also have to fight to gain critical acceptance of their artistic expression. Others would expand upon the abstraction of and attention to isolated movement, but modern dance would eventually not only reconcile with ballet, but would also incorporate many other dance styles into its palette. Prominent modern dancers include the well-known names of Hanya Holm, Martha Graham, Doris Humphrey, Charles Weidman, and Merce Cunningham. Their influence continues to the present day; these pioneers set the stage for modern dance to become a viable art in the twenty-first century.

—Elizabeth A. Hanley
Associate Professor Emerita of Kinesiology at
Pennsylvania State University

FOREWORD

In song and dance, man expresses himself as a member of a higher community. He forgets how to walk and speak and is on the way into flying into the air, dancing. . . . his very gestures express enchantment.

—Friedrich Nietzsche

In a conversation with George Balanchine (one of the twentieth century's most famous choreographers and the cofounder of the New York City Ballet) discussing the definition of dance, we evolved the following description: "Dance is an expression of time and space, using the control of movement and gesture to communicate."

Dance is central to the human being's expression of emotion. Every time we shake someone's hand, lift a glass in a toast, wave good-bye, or applaud a performer—we are doing a form of dance. We live in a universe of time and space, and dance is an art form invented by human beings to express and convey emotions. Dance is profound.

There are melodies that, when played, will cause your heart to droop with sadness for no known reason. Or a rousing jig or mazurka will have your foot tapping in an accompanying rhythm, seemingly beyond your control. The emotions, contacted through music, spur the body to react physically. Our bodies have just been programmed to express emotions. We dance for many reasons: for religious rituals from the most ancient times; for dealing with sadness, tearfully swaying and holding hands at a wake; for celebrating weddings, joyfully spinning in circles; for entertainment; for dating and mating. How many millions of couples through the ages have said, "We met at a dance"? But most of all, we dance for joy, often exclaiming, "How I love to dance!" Oh, the JOY OF DANCE!

I was teaching dance at a boarding school for emotionally disturbed children, ages 9 through 16. They were participating with 20 other schools in the National Dance Institute's (NDI) year-round program. The boarding school children had been traumatized in frightening and mind-boggling ways. There were a dozen students in my class, and the average attention span may have been 15 seconds—which made for a raucous bunch. This was a tough class.

One young boy, an 11-year-old, was an exception. He never took his eyes off of me for the 35 minutes of the dance class, and they were blazing blue eyes—electric, set in a chalk-white face. His body was slim, trim, superbly proportioned, and he stood arrow-straight. His lips were clamped in a rigid, determined line as he learned and executed every dance step with amazing skill. His concentration was intense despite the wild cavorting, noise, and otherwise disruptive behavior supplied by his fellow classmates.

At the end of class I went up to him and said, "Wow, can you dance. You're great! What's your name?"

Those blue eyes didn't blink. Then he parted his ridged lips and bared his teeth in a grimace that may have been a smile. He had a big hole where his front teeth should be. I covered my shock and didn't let it show. Both top and bottom incisors had been worn away by his continual grinding and rubbing of them together. One of the supervisors of the school rushed over to me and said, "Oh, his name is Michael. He's very intelligent, but he doesn't speak."

I heard Michael's story from the supervisor. Apparently, when he was a toddler in his playpen, he witnessed his father shooting his mother; then, putting the gun to his own head, the father killed himself. It was close to three days before the neighbors broke in to find the dead and swollen bodies of his parents. The dehydrated and starving little boy was stuck in his playpen, sitting in his own filth. The orphaned Michael disappeared into the foster care system, eventually ending up in the boarding school. No one had ever heard him speak.

In the ensuing weeks of dance class, I built and developed choreography for Michael and his classmates. In the spring, they were scheduled to dance in a spectacular NDI show called *The Event of the Year*. At the boarding school, I used Michael as the leader and as a model for the others and began welding all of the kids together, inventing a vigorous and energetic dance to utilize their explosive energy. It took awhile, but they were coming together, little by little over the months. And through all that time, the best in the class—the determined and concentrating Michael—never spoke.

That spring, dancers from the 22 different schools with which the NDI had dance programs were scheduled to come together at Madison Square Garden for *The Event of the Year*. There would be more than 2,000 dancers, a symphony orchestra, a jazz orchestra, a chorus, Broadway stars, narrators, and Native American Indian drummers. There was scenery that was the length of an entire city block and visiting guest children from six foreign countries coming to dance with our New York City children. All of these elements had to come together and fit into a spectacular performance, with only one day of rehearsal. The foremost challenge was how to get 2,000 dancing children on stage for the opening number.

At NDI, we have developed a system called "the runs." First, we divide the stage into a grid with colored lines making the outlines of box shapes, making a mosaic of patterns and shapes on the stage floor. Each outlined box holds a class from one of the schools, which consists of 15 to 30 children. Then, we add various colored lines as tracks, starting offstage and leading to the boxes. The dancers line up in the wings, hallways, and various holding areas on either side of the stage. At the end of the overture, they burst onto the stage, running and leaping and following their colored tracks to their respective boxes, where they explode into the opening dance number.

We had less than three minutes to accomplish "the runs." It's as if a couple of dozen trains coming from different places and traveling on different tracks all arrived at a station at the same time, safely pulling into their allotted spaces. But even before starting, it would take us almost an hour just to get the dancers lined up in the correct holding areas offstage, ready to make their entrance. We had scheduled one shot to rehearse the opening. It had to work the first time or we would have to repeat everything. That meant going into overtime at a great expense.

I gave the cue to start the number. The orchestra, singers, lights, and stagehands all commenced on cue, and the avalanche of 2,000 children were let loose on their tracks. "The runs" had begun!

After about a minute, I realized something was wrong. There was a big pileup on stage left and children were colliding into each other and bunching up behind some obstacle. I ran over to discover the source of the problem: Michael and his classmates. He had ignored everything and led the group from his school right up front, as close to the audience as he could get. Inspiring his dancing buddies, they were a crew of leaping, contorting demons—dancing up a storm, but blocking some 600 other dancers trying to get through.

I rushed up to them, yelling, "You're in the wrong place! Back up! Back up!"

Michael—with his eyes blazing, mouth open, and legs and arms spinning in dance movements like an eggbeater—yelled out, "Oh, I am so happy! I am so happy! Thank you, Jacques! Oh, it's so good! I am so happy!"

I backed off, stunned into silence. I sat down in the first row of the audience and was joined by several of the supervisors, teachers, and chaperones from Michael's school, our mouths open in wonder. The spirit of dance had taken over Michael and his classmates. No one danced better or with more passion in the whole show that night and with Michael leading the way—the JOY OF DANCE was at work. (We went into overtime, but so what!)

—Jacques D'Amboise
Author of *Teaching the Magic of Dance*, winner of an
Academy Award for *He Makes Me Feel Like Dancin'*,
and Founder of the National Dance Institute

The Precursors

My art is just an effort to express the truth of my being in gesture and movement.[1]

—Isadora Duncan

When visitors to the Paris Exposition of 1900 crowded into the Palais de Danse to gape at exotic Egyptian belly dancers or Turkish whirling dervishes, they did so in a building crowned by a statue of American dancer Loie Fuller. In order to see Fuller herself dance, one had to enter the vine-carved entrance of the little Art Nouveau theater, Le Théâtre de la Loie Fuller, which was dedicated to presenting "La Loie" (as she was known in France) and her protégées. Moving in a blur of scarves and draperies, which she manipulated with sticks, Fuller transformed herself into flowers, butterflies, and fire, as colored lights projected from her own small electric dynamo played across her swirling figure. The effect was magical, and her audiences gasped and cheered. Using electricity, the most advanced technology of her time, as well as some Yankee ingenuity, Fuller turned her dancing form into a living abstraction.

LOIE FULLER: A SPARK OF ENERGY

No one could identify what Fuller was doing, although artists and writers across Europe tried to capture her in motion. She seemed to be the embodiment of the progress that the exhibition was celebrating—a living, breathing spark of electricity. Nothing was newer than harnessed electric power, and nothing else seemed to hold more promise for the future in 1900. Loie Fuller's whirling form was not new simply because her dance symbolized the larger scientific interests of her era. More than an exotic oddity performing at a world's fair, she was a dancer as radically different and as fueled by new energies as the industrial accomplishments on view at the exposition.

Fuller was one of the sparks that lit the fire we call **modern dance**. Two other dancers, Isadora Duncan and Ruth St. Denis, each performing independently of the other, added their own fuel to the early flames. These American women, each following a self-determined method of dancing, were its precursors. Of course, they did not set out to do any such thing; nor did they call their art "modern dance." All these three women wanted to do was to express themselves as dancers in a highly personal way. Individually and separately, they rejected **ballet** or theatrical show dancing, the only two concert forms of dance acceptable at the beginning of the twentieth century, when their careers flourished. Their dancing was connected only by their will to experiment, for what they performed on stage could not have been more different from the other.

La Loie literally stumbled into her dance innovation. The oldest of the three dancers, Fuller was born in Illinois in 1862, but hers was not a typical Midwestern childhood. She performed on stages as a child actress and grew up in theater, later moving from Chicago to New York. In 1890, while rehearsing for a play, she kept tripping over the voluminous material of her costume. Eventually, she cleverly placed sticks under her skirt, allowing her the practical accomplishment of being able to lift the fabric off the floor and thus avoid falling down on stage. Quite unexpectedly, she found that moving her garments in this way

American dancer Loie Fuller thrilled audiences in France during the Paris Exposition in 1900. This poster for the Folies Bergère, created by famed poster artist Jules Chéret, promotes Fuller's talents for an upcoming performance at the Parisian music hall.

glamorously extended the movement of her own body and captivated the audience.

Shifting one's skirts around on stage was an actual genre of dance at that time and was called, appropriately enough, "skirt dancing." The dancer would swing and lift her skirts, perhaps adding some acrobatics, and call it Greek, Oriental, Egyptian, or whatever suited her. It is likely that the then-titillating glimpses of petticoats and even an ankle now and then are what gave the form popularity, for it certainly represented no high artistic aspiration.

There were no ballet companies in the United States at that time, nor any schools of professional dance. Stage dancing usually meant show-girls performing largely self-taught kicks and turns. Beyond that, personal expression in movement usually referred to complicated physical-culture theories, especially **eurythmics**, a system of harmonious body movements first put forward by Émile Jaques-Dalcroze (better known as "**Dalcroze**"). At best, this system taught gymnastics through response to music, and at its worst degenerated into pretentious calisthenics programs. Skirt dancing at least provided an outlet for the would-be dance experimenters who used the form in innovative ways.

Fuller perfected her dance illusion touring across the United States, where her effects were admired as good entertainment. Europeans, on the other hand, saw her as something more than a touring oddity. Settling in Paris, Fuller found herself celebrated as an artist, and she became a fixture at the famous extravaganza the Folies Bergère. Loie became the toast of the Parisian art community long before she triumphed at the Paris Exposition.

Artists and writers saw her transform herself into abstract patterns moving on stage, the living expression of artistic ideas sweeping Paris and the world. The ripple of fabric that she sent into the air seemed to mimic the sinuous decorative-art movement known as Art Nouveau of the late nineteenth and early twentieth centuries. This "New Art" emphasized line, whiplash curve, and the arabesque. Its long, curving lines were considered to be organic and therefore reflecting nature. Artists employed these curving forms for everything from the famous Paris Metro signs to posters. A Parisian critic noted that when Fuller danced, she was "sculptured by the air, the cloth rose and fell, swelled and contracted . . . recalling the fluid lines of Art Nouveau designers."[2]

The Post-Impressionist artist Henri Toulouse-Lautrec, famous for his Art Nouveau-influenced posters of the Paris nightlife establishments he frequented, portrayed Fuller in a lithograph. Upon first glance, she looks like a huge cloud floating in space; only tiny feet under the soaring abstraction reveal this as a woman dancing. Other artists tried to capture Fuller's magic, including sculptor Pierre Roche, whose small bronzes made Fuller look like a beautiful, exotic flower. Even the great sculptor Rodin—whose own work, such as his famous sculpture *The Thinker*, celebrated the human body—was interested in sculpting Fuller. Although nothing came of this, he did call her "a woman of genius."[3]

Both Isadora Duncan and Ruth St. Denis saw Fuller perform at the Paris Exposition. Although Fuller's extravagant performance was quite far removed from their own emotionally and spiritually conceived dances, they admired her nonetheless. Duncan said of seeing Loie perform, "Before our very eyes she turned to many coloured, shining orchids, to a wavering, flowing sea flower, and at length to a spiral-like lily, all the magic of Merlin, the sorcery of light, colour, flowing form. What an extraordinary genius."[4]

Although she founded a school and staged group productions, Fuller's art was too uniquely her own to survive without her constant attention. When she died, her magic largely died with her. Yet, Irish poet William Butler Yeats wrote of seeing her: [5]

> When Loie Fuller's Chinese dancers enwound
> A shining web, a floating ribbon of cloth
> It seemed that a dragon of air
> Had fallen among dancers, had whirled them round . . . .

Fuller's high theatricality and her submergence of self in costume and light to create a movement effect opened up new areas of theater to dancers. The respect she gained as an innovator created an artistic climate where other innovators could flourish. The skirt dance was about to disappear, but Duncan and St. Denis would be burdened with this characterization before they banished it forever.

(continues on page 21)

DANCE AS ILLUSION

When Loie Fuller twirled her long scarves and costumes while colored lights rippled over her, she wasn't just introducing new movement ideas using emerging technology—she was creating an illusion. In the more than 100 years since La Loie created this innovation, many other dancer-choreographers have used fabric and technology to create dance illusions.

At a very deep level, all dance is an illusion. After all, none of the rest of us can dance on our toes or leap across a stage and land in a perfect position. Like athletes, skilled dancers are physically able to demonstrate to an audience the range of possibilities contained within our own human form. Yet, Loie was not interested in demonstrating her athletic skills; she wanted to create something beautiful out of movement, fabric, and technology, which in her case meant a small electric dynamo projecting colored lights onto her costumes.

Over time, other choreographers have used the same formula. In 1982, David Parsons created a solo for himself called *Caught*. He performs on a dark stage with a strobe light that hits different parts of the stage every few seconds, and then the stage goes dark briefly. The dancer leaps and is "caught" at the top of his leap just as each round of the strobe light goes off. This means the strobe light has been programmed to go off at a certain spot at a certain time, and it also means that the dancer must be on the count so that when the light goes on he is at the top of his leap. Thus the audience only sees him as he repeatedly and quickly appears in the air. As he circles the stage, he gives the appearance of flying, sitting on air, and then at the end—thump, he lands. To this day, *Caught* remains a spectacular performance piece, a dazzling tour de force showing what movement and technology can do in the computer era.

Fabric continues to be a useful stage device for dancers. Perhaps the greatest of Alvin Ailey's dance works is his *Revelations*, performed to African-American gospel music. One of the show-stopping segments of this work is *Wade in the Waters*, in which long pieces of fabric stretched across the stage are rippled and rolled like water. The dancers holding parasols over their heads daintily step over each rippling wave to reach the safe shore. Creating the illusion of water on stage with this simple device has been used many times but rarely as effectively.

No choreographer took more interest in the fabric used to costume and set the scene for her work than Martha Graham. She actually picked out specific fabric for each of her works, personally selecting stretch fabrics, tricots, and elasticized synthetics. Then she would drape them herself, a skill she learned from her days with famed dancer Ruth St. Denis in the Denishawn dance troupe. For her solo *Lamentation*, she wrapped herself totally in a jersey tube so that all an audience saw were the shapes made by her body moving inside this tube. It remains a masterpiece.

Pilobolus is a dance company that chooses illusion as its primary choreographic device. With simple backlighting, the dancers bodies twine together in a way that can create the illusion of a plant, a table, or even a giraffe. Children use this same technique when they make shadow images with their hands. It is a rare dance company in the twenty-first century that does not use computerized backdrop images. For *Amjad*, the Quebec dance group La La La Human Steps features continuously changing black and white nature photographs that extend the illustration of the dances. Technology has changed music accompaniment, as well, with the introduction of synthesized music and computerized sound tracks. Loie's small electric dynamo started it all.

Pictured here posing for a studio portrait, Isadora Duncan was one of the founders of modern dance. Duncan admired Loie Fuller and, like her predecessor, was praised throughout Europe.

(continued from page 17)

ISADORA DUNCAN: MOVEMENT COMES FROM EMOTION

Isadora Duncan's story was in some ways similar to Fuller's. She too became world famous and was then known simply by her first name. She also was admired by Rodin, although his admiration included unwanted amorous advances. There was, however, nothing accidental about Duncan's dancing or her career. Encouraged to dance by her artistic mother, Duncan was a lonely child, growing up in a family that was socially shunned because of her father's financial troubles and her parents' subsequent divorce. Duncan turned inward, saying later that she began dancing in her mother's womb. She certainly had complete confidence in her own intuitive movements from her earliest days. As a teenager, she and her siblings would teach neighborhood children to dance. Said Duncan of her earliest instruction, "We called it a new system of dancing but in reality there was no system. I followed my fantasy and improvised."[6]

For Duncan, movement sprang out of emotion. This is, in fact, the fundamental notion of the Duncan style. The dancer needs to go into his or her very center and produce a pure movement in response to specific feeling. This had nothing to do with technique. There were no positions to learn or steps to memorize, and Duncan avoided special lighting or stage effects. "My art," she said, "is just an effort to express the truth of my being in gesture and movement."[7]

Early in her life, Duncan focused on the idea of becoming a serious concert dancer while using her own style of movement. As a teenager accompanied by her family, she went first to Chicago and then on to New York looking for work as a dancer. Without much difficulty, she found jobs in musical revues, but she felt these positions were not true to her theory of dancing. Seeking to express pure emotion through movement, Duncan looked for a place where she could perform. She was forced to take her serious, introspective solo dances into society ladies' salons, where she was politely applauded. But Duncan wanted recognition as an artist, not as a parlor entertainer. Seeking a more appreciative audience, Duncan and her accommodating family went first to London and then to Paris, where, like Loie Fuller, she found great success and a new home.

Isadora Duncan must have been a sight to behold. Her emotive dance was performed wearing loose tunics (and later, beautifully draped Grecian robes), and she usually danced without shoes. She performed on bare stages in front of a simple blue backdrop to the accompaniment of highly dramatic classical music—Beethoven and Wagner being particular favorites—or in absolute silence. She looked—as indeed she had intended to—as though she had stepped out of an ancient fresco of dancing goddesses. She often paused to tell the audience her views on current events, creating a sense that the entire production was improvised. This, however, was not true, as her dances were carefully crafted, although changed and modified in any given performance. They are re-created even today by her still-dedicated followers.

Duncan was an original who really was touched by genius. Careful reconstructions of her famous dances show us nothing of the power she had individually as a performer. As dancer/choreographer Agnes de Mille observed, "Her greatest technical contribution—her personal performance—tends to be forgotten because it cannot be copied."[8]

Loie Fuller saw Duncan dance in Paris, and the two dancers admired each other's work. Fuller arranged for Duncan to join a tour to Berlin. The Germans in particular were taken by Duncan's approach to dancing, as they had embraced the movement systems popular at the time, particularly those of Dalcroze's eurythmics. (Isadora's more personal, emotion-based theories of dance were not strictly the same as those of Dalcroze and his followers. However, both styles could look the same since each relied on an easily moving, well-balanced body using simple gestures to express emotion.) So enthusiastic were the Germans about Duncan's innovative dancing that she chose to establish her first school teaching the Isadora Duncan dance method in Berlin in 1905.

In personal matters, however, Duncan had a dramatic and unhappy life. She became a passionate feminist as a result of seeing her mother struggle to support her family while being scorned for her divorce. When Duncan had two children of her own, she chose not to marry their father. Her pleasure in her children was short-lived as they drowned in a freakish automobile accident in Paris in 1913, when the car plunged into the river Seine. Duncan sank into despair, and her dances at that time, such as *March Slav*, reflect this emotional state.

Admiring the Bolshevik revolution in Russia, Duncan defended the newly Communist Soviet Russia, eventually even moving to Russia, where she established yet another European dance institute in 1921 in Moscow. She was completely oblivious to critics who labeled her a Communist, even composing dances to be performed at Lenin's funeral. After avoiding the convention of marriage for her entire life, Duncan surprised everyone in 1922 by marrying the young Russian poet Sergey Yesenin, who was 17 years her junior. An impoverished Duncan eventually left Russia in 1924 after her school lost government support and her husband had committed suicide.

Tragedies and setbacks, however, never affected Duncan for long. She returned to France and began giving dance performances again, demonstrating that her charisma was undiminished by age. Her comeback triumph did not last long, unfortunately. A bizarre automobile accident claimed her life in 1927, when she dramatically tossed a scarf around her neck as she got into a sports car. Caught in the wheel spokes, the scarf broke her neck when the car moved forward. She had more to tell the world, however; her autobiography appeared almost immediately following her death.

Isadora Duncan never set out to be part of a reform movement in dance. She considered her art to be true dance—genius, in fact—and what everyone else did was simply theatrical silliness. She intellectualized her movements while claiming they sprang from emotions. The notion of dance as expression of inner states of being was Isadora's gift to what became modern dance. This was a very new concept indeed. Certainly no skirt dancer before her had ever made such extravagant claims.

RUTH ST. DENIS: DANCE AS A SPIRITUAL PURSUIT

If Duncan turned to emotion as movement's source, her contemporary Ruth St. Denis looked to what she called the spirit. Born Ruth Dennis in 1879 in New Jersey, she changed her name in the early years of her

Known for her portrayal of Eastern cultures in her dance, Ruth St. Denis gained notoriety while on America's vaudeville circuit. She is pictured here during a solo performance in the 1890s.

career when she danced in musical revues. A producer called her "Saint Dennis" as a way of teasing her about her high-minded and serious approach to dance. She liked the sound of St. Denis, and it was true that for her, dance was a spiritual pursuit. "As I see it," she said, "the deepest lack of Western cultures is any true workable system for teaching a process of integration between soul and body."[9]

Like Fuller and Duncan before her, St. Denis's earliest stage appearances were in popular musical theater. While on tour in 1904, she happened to see a cigarette advertisement with an image of the Egyptian goddess Isis. This image so captured her imagination that she became determined to create dances in the Oriental manner—that is, a Western notion of Eastern cultures that was more romanticized than authentic. She eventually became receptive to the entire spectrum of spiritual thought that she associated with the Near East and Far East.

St. Denis was a beautiful, mesmerizing performer like Duncan and Fuller, but she was less fussy about where she danced. Although she toured in Europe, St. Denis's professional life unfolded in the United States, and she actually created her first major success, *Radha*, with the vaudeville circuit in mind. *Radha* was her solo dance, and she portrayed a Hindu temple idol. She was so hypnotizing as she slithered off her temple pedestal to explore the temptations of the senses that it hardly mattered that her steps were a hodgepodge of ballet turns, acrobatics in the eurythmic tradition, and poses that froze the lovely St. Denis into Oriental images directly out of nothing more authentic than her own imagination. No one cared that the set was not a Jain temple or that the music by Delibes had been composed for a European opera. This formula would be reinvented throughout St. Denis's career as she singly— and eventually with a company—brought the entire world of mysticism and Oriental religious practices as she envisioned it to stages of all sizes throughout the country.

In 1914, influenced by the enormous success of the ballroom dancers Irene and Vernon Castle (who were then at the height of their fame), St. Denis decided to find a male partner. But she was more interested in the performing tension between male and female partners than ballroom dance. She selected Ted Shawn, a former divinity student, who had trained in ballet for therapeutic reasons. He was a handsome man with a physique that people compared to that of a Greek god. Spiritually a seeker as well and physically the male equal of her beauty, he was an ideal match for St. Denis. Together they became Denishawn.

Denishawn shifts the story of modern dance away from the precursors. St. Denis and Shawn created more than a dance company—they started a dance school, brought men into dance innovation, and eventually created one of the most important dance festivals in the world. They were innovators who were not uncomfortable creating institutions that would secure a place for modern dance in theater arts. Fuller and Duncan had been worshipped during their lifetimes, but only St. Denis lived long enough to hear herself called the mother of modern dance.

Denishawn

Dance . . . the symbol and language for communicating spiritual truth.

—Ruth St. Denis[10]

When Ruth St. Denis married Ted Shawn in 1914, neither could have imagined the dance legacy their union would produce. At the time, it seemed a straightforward partnership of two attractive dancers who both needed something the other had to give. St. Denis wanted a male dance partner, and Shawn, who had long admired St. Denis's spiritual approach to dance, wanted to learn from her. The two shared long-term dreams of a school and dance communities that would be centered on utopian ideals. Almost immediately, they began a conversation about such goals. If the introspective St. Denis tended to see these possibilities as spiritual directions, the ever-practical Shawn started to implement them almost at once.

A NEW SCHOOL OF MODERN DANCE

Billed as "Ruth St. Denis, assisted by Ted Shawn, with Hilda Beyer" (his dance partner at that time), St. Denis and Shawn began touring. Not long after they had started working together and just as World War I was declared, they married on August 13, 1914. St. Denis was 36 and Shawn was just 23. Prematurely white-haired, St. Denis was a regal figure, and Shawn, at more than six feet tall, made a noble consort. The name *Denishawn* was actually not of their design but rather the result of an enterprising theater owner's promotion. It stuck, although the company that began with their partnership would continue to be billed as "Ruth St. Denis" until 1921.

Romantic as the combined name sounds, there was a tension between the couple from the start. St. Denis, the dreamer, and Shawn, the realist, were often at odds. Depending on the observer's point of view, Shawn either was St. Denis's perfect complement or someone who used her to further his own ambition. Agnes de Mille, the great dancer/choreographer who knew both dancers, observed much later:

> He [Shawn] refers to her as though she were his guru. But she was not his guru, she was his middle-aged wife, famous while he was unknown, sought after while he was passed by, worshipped by dancers while he was tolerated as their equal, envied only as having special and unfair advantages. In short, she was a genuine star while he was a pretender. She was also a woman of genuine convictions; what he had were genuine ambitions.[11]

Others were less unkind. Jane Sherman, a member of the Denishawn troupe who worked closely with the two for years, observed more mildly that, "[s]he supplied the glamour and inspiration, he the organization and teaching drive."[12]

In any event, the 1915 opening of the Ruth St. Denis School of Dancing on a wooded hilltop in Los Angeles was a major milestone—not just in the lives of these two dancers but also in the history of American dance. By the next year, the name was changed to the Denishawn School, thus officially acknowledging the joint nature of their endeavors. For St. Denis, the school was a place of final repose in a lifetime of touring, providing

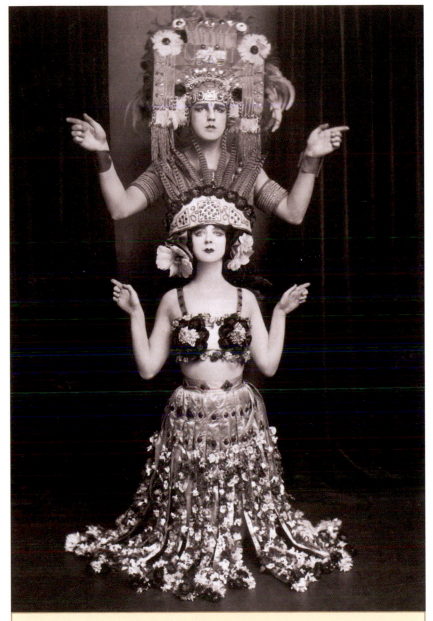

Ted Shawn (*top*) and Ruth St. Denis (*bottom*) pose in costumes for a performance of a dance entitled *Xochitl*.

her a base from which to practice and reaffirm her spiritual beliefs. She had limited interest in teaching, however, and focused her energies primarily on performance. She had been dancing professionally long before achieving real success in 1906's *Radha*, when she was 27 years old. The huge success of this "Indian" dance propelled her into years of touring in vaudeville and performing in private engagements.

As St. Denis's repertory had expanded to Egyptian and Japanese themes, she used dancers on an as-needed basis to fill out larger dances. When she mounted her full-length *Egypta* with a cast of 50 in 1910, the dancers were hired for the tour, and the elaborate costumes and sets of this dance-theater piece had to be created for ease in transport. Thus, the establishment of a school with facilities for training dancers, as well as for creating and storing sets and costumes, was no small gift from a young husband to a revered older wife. The Los Angeles facility was joined later by the addition of a major Denishawn center in New York City and countless branches across the United States. Shawn made it possible for his charismatic wife to become universally known and admired as "Miss Ruth," and he helped show future generations that it was possible to financially support their creative concert work on a foundation of teaching and touring.

The goal of the school was "the eternal quest for truth, the ecstasy of an instant's communication with a divine being, the harmony of rituals, beautifully performed."[13] If Shawn's drive brought the school into being, it was St. Denis's vision that kept Denishawn set on a course of high purpose, where spiritual goals would be pursued in partnership with performing. It would be a place where Miss Ruth could hold seminars on Oriental mysticism and religion, at least as it was known in the West at that time. The seminars provided a heady infusion of breathing exercises, meditation, Hindu philosophy, and even Christian Science practices.

St. Denis did not teach dance, although she instructed on facial expressions and gestures. Shawn and a small teaching staff introduced students to a variety of Oriental dances as well as ballet and general movement exercises, based primarily on the **Delsarte** method of "natural" movement theory. The school managed to advertise itself as something of a finishing school, which attracted the daughters and sons of the middle class. However, the school's prosperous neighbors, residing in secluded and beautifully landscaped homes nearby, found the undertaking dangerously arty. Every incident, such as the young women of Denishawn dashing down the school's suburban street in bathing suits trying to retrieve the resident peacock, managed to be reported in the newspaper. To this island of serene introspection and emotive movement high in the Los Angeles hills came dancers from all over. Some stayed for a session or two and drifted away, while others became members of the Denishawn touring company. Three of them would eventually split away from Denishawn to form their own companies—thus actually beginning modern dance as we know it.

In 1916, in the second summer of the school's existence, the first of the three visionary dancers, Martha Graham, entered the school in spite of Miss Ruth's initial impression that she was "totally hopeless"[14] and the fact that Graham was considered to be short, dumpy, and untrained. Doris Humphrey arrived from Chicago in 1917 with the goal of simply teaching dance, and in her case, Miss Ruth approved, saying to her, "You should dance."[15] At about the same time, Charles Weidman arrived from Lincoln, Nebraska, where he had seen Denishawn on tour.

One other key figure in the history of modern dance was also in the group. Louis Horst was Denishawn's musical director from 1915 to 1925 and would go on to accompany, compose for, and collaborate with succeeding generations of modern-dance innovators. The impact of this quartet lay in the future; for the next 15 years, their lives would be intertwined with Denishawn, and their personal visions would be submerged in its high exoticism.

The Spread of Denishawn

Unlike Loie Fuller and Isadora Duncan, St. Denis and Shawn were interested in finding an audience in the United States. To do this, they took the company to the small towns and burgeoning cities of the 48 states. They did not despise the vaudeville circuit as Duncan and Fuller had, nor did they feel that their artistic integrity was in any way threatened. The only truly respectable stage for dance was at the New York Metropolitan Opera House, but opportunities there were very limited and mostly restricted to ballet dancers filling out crowd scenes in opera productions.

To most Americans, vaudeville simply meant a variety show presented in a theater. Small theaters across the United States were built by enterprising owners who created chains, while others were individually owned. The term *vaudeville* comes from the French term *vaux-de-ville*, used in France as early as the eighteenth century to describe a theatrical entertainment with a variety of acts. But by the 1880s, vaudeville was universally accepted in the United States as a variety show that could consist of dancers, comedians, singers, acrobats, animal acts, and just about any stage novelty imaginable. When motion pictures first became popular, vaudeville acts often preceded or followed the film presentation. For almost 80 years, vaudeville provided the average American access to entertainment and culture.

Ruth St. Denis had first presented *Radha*, the dance that made her famous, at Worth's Family Theater and Museum in New York. Here, she danced six times a day on a program of variety acts in a setting that was shared with displays of pickled animal freaks and between lectures on historical relics, which were also on view. So, going from one theater to another as a featured act of a theater chain did not seem all that terrible. St. Denis could also leave the tedious task of bookings or arranging tour logistics to the impresario hiring her troupe.

DENISHAWN TAKES OFF

As the Denishawn company grew in size, augmented continually by dancers training at its own school, the company's productions became grander. Each program included several St. Denis solos, which might be anything from her famous cobras, in which her arms became serpents, to Yogi, just one of her many dance meditations based on Eastern religious practices. St. Denis and Shawn began performing in new works that showcased their combined talent in duets ranging from ballroom dance to mystical and exotic creations such as *The Garden of Kama*, a love story between a highborn Indian beauty and a fisherman. The program also included full-company dances and usually one or two short "musical visualizations," which St. Denis described as "the scientific translation into bodily action of the rhythmic, melodic, and harmonious structure of musical composition." St. Denis readily said that Isadora Duncan had inspired her to approach music in this way. Through the years, Shawn began to be showcased in solo work as well, and later, his own full-company **choreography** was performed. Each of these was a short work that could be interspersed throughout a program with other acts.

An opportunity to work on a large scale came to Denishawn in 1916 in the form of an invitation to perform at the Greek Theatre of the University of California at Berkeley. Denishawn was the first dance company so honored. St. Denis used the entire school to create a dance pageant of Egyptian, Greek, and Indian styles, including having the students dye and stencil cloth as well as sew some of the 450 costumes. In addition to the Denishawn students, St. Denis used almost 100 dancers from the Berkeley summer session.

St. Denis's dream of recapturing the spirit of ancient performance was nearly realized in the Berkeley commission. Later in life, she said, "The experience of these rehearsals is among the high points of my career." She mused happily over the long hours of rehearsal with trunks of costumes open in the sunshine and the pleasant sounds of hammering going on backstage, where sets and props were being constructed. All the while, visitors strolled by watching the preparations. She had felt then as though "the antique world hovered in the radiant sunshine. We could have been in a Greek theater in the ancient land."[16]

Each of the pageant sections portrayed daily life and spiritual pursuits of the three selected civilizations of Egypt, Greece, and India. An actual river of water created along a broad walk at the front of the stage successively represented the Nile, the Styx, and, finally, the Ganges. One of St. Denis and Shawn's most enduring dance duets, *Toilers of the Soil*, appeared first in the Egyptian section. In *Toilers*, the pair moved in profile like hieroglyphic figures as they went about their daily tasks of plowing, planting, and harvesting. Shawn's head was shaved and he wore a loincloth, while St. Denis was draped in a shapeless, sacklike garment. This dance is one of the very few to survive on film, and although both dancers were more than 60 years old at the time it was filmed, Shawn's balletic training and poise still is apparent, as is St. Denis's mesmerizing ability to suggest character and thought in movement. The pageant was later performed at the Panama California Exposition in San Diego, as well as in Los Angeles and Santa Barbara. Its individual dances, such as *Toilers in the Soil*, would enter into the permanent Denishawn repertory.

Although a huge artistic success, the pageant left Denishawn in debt. As St. Denis said, the only real answer to this problem was vaudeville. "This contingency always disturbed Ted more than it did me," she said. "He sometimes questioned whether this means of freeing ourselves from debt was worth the loss in artistic prestige, which he believed accompanied a two-a-day. But to me debt loomed as a greater moral defeat than any hypothetical loss of prestige."[17]

One other avenue of popular work supported Denishawn: the burgeoning movie industry that was then taking root in Los Angeles. The sumptuous, epic nature of Denishawn found its counterpart in the silent movies then being produced by Cecil B. de Mille (whose niece, Agnes de Mille, would become a dancer/choreographer) and D.W. Griffith. Both virtually invented the screen epic with films such as *The Ten Commandments* and *The Birth of a Nation*. Many Denishawn dancers and students ended up in motion pictures, including Julianne Johnston, who starred with Douglas Fairbanks in *The Thief of Baghdad*. Silent-screen great Louise Brooks, herself a film icon, was also a Denishawn dancer. D.W. Griffith actually required his actresses to attend Denishawn classes to learn how to convey emotion through movement. St. Denis choreographed a Babylonian dance for Griffith's huge film *Intolerance*, calling on Denishawn students to appear in it.

Touring, however, paid the bills. Following the pageant's success in 1916, the troupe spent the rest of that year and much of 1917 performing on the Orpheum vaudeville circuit. With America's entrance into World War I and Shawn's enlistment in the United States Army Ambulance Corps, St. Denis toured vaudeville on her own once again. When the war ended and Shawn returned, Denishawn was promptly out touring the Pantages vaudeville circuit in 1919. During this time, Shawn himself

Movie star Louise Brooks, who appeared in 17 silent films during her acting career, was also a prominent member of the Denishawn dance troupe. Brooks (*center*) is pictured in the late 1920s.

began experimenting as a choreographer. He took the exploration of American Indian myth and tradition as his personal territory in such dances as *Xochitl*, which gave Martha Graham her first star turn as a feisty Toltec maiden.

Year after year, the dancers were on the road doing two-a-day performances on the vaudeville circuit, which one former dancer described as "uninspiring, almost degrading labor."[18] It was not uncommon for Denishawn, even with its high-art aspirations, to appear on a program with comedian Fanny Brice as the next act. Denishawn even had the honor of playing New York's Palace, vaudeville's greatest stage, where they were so popular that their performances were extended for a second week. The high point of their life on the road came in 1925 and 1926 with a prestigious tour through the Orient, taking their Western imitations of Eastern religion and myth to the source itself. They visited eight countries, including Japan, China, and India. The tour was a triumph, with Eastern audiences more appreciative of the implied compliment than critical of any irregularities or errors in Denishawn's vision of them. The troupe returned home exhausted, only to go back on the road immediately, spending 40 weeks in 1927 and 1928 touring with the Ziegfeld Follies.

DENISHAWN UNRAVELS

By then, the pressure of touring was taking its toll on everyone in the company. Drawn to Denishawn by a desire to perform serious, high-art dance, the troupe felt wearied, and sometimes even sullied, by the grueling demands of touring and the often makeshift environments where they performed. Shawn and St. Denis's relationship was strained by this as well. St. Denis was never comfortable as a married woman, resisting the notion of an ordinary domestic life, a family, and a home. Meanwhile, Shawn pushed for more control over Denishawn as well as visibility for his own dance works. He also was a fervent pioneer in the effort to lure men back to serious dance after a long period during which dancing was considered—especially in the United States—to be something that only women did. St. Denis wanted time to reflect and to recoup, but Shawn, ever full of energy, was bursting with new ideas for the company. Both partners had flirtations with other people, and there were rumors that Shawn's were with other men, something vehemently denied at a time when homosexuality actually was illegal in much of the United States. Shawn summed up his own view of the situation when he wearily titled one of his books *One Thousand and One Night Stands*.

Martha Graham was the first dancer to defect, but others such as Doris Humphrey and Charles Weidman would follow, going on to become the great founding generation of independent modern-dance artists. Less inevitable but perhaps even more damaging was the departure of Louis

JACOB'S PILLOW DANCE FESTIVAL

In 1930, Ted Shawn bought a farm in Massachusetts to use as a retreat. The farm could be reached only by a windy road that locals called The Ladder. Behind the farmhouse was a huge boulder with a sunken middle that looked like a pillow. Pious New Englanders who had built the farm called it Jacob's Pillow, because it suggested to them the Book of Genesis passage in which Jacob laid his head on a rock and dreamed of a ladder leading to heaven.

Jacob's Pillow would become Denishawn's gift to the dance community and longest-lasting achievement, although this came about quite accidentally. In 1933, Shawn brought together eight men—some of whom were physical education students at a nearby college—to create a new kind of male-based dance performance. He wanted to establish a strong masculine style that would convince audiences that dance was not something for ladies only. While he was training these young men in dance arts, he also kept them in shape by using them to build the compound of structures that exist at Jacob's Pillow to this day.

For seven years, Shawn and His Men Dancers (as they were called) toured worldwide, always returning to Jacob's Pillow for summer performances and lectures open to the

Horst, Denishawn's musical director. Unlike dancers, who—at least in theory—could easily be replaced within the Denishawn system, Horst was fundamental to the acts of choreographing and producing. There were no other composer-musicians training in Denishawn workshops.

Agnes de Mille called Graham's departure "the first wound in the flesh of Denishawn,"[19] saying Graham "spurned" Shawn in particular. Graham herself described her leaving more prosaically, saying,

public. Although Shawn and Ruth St. Denis were separated by this point, Miss Ruth always was invited to perform. World War II changed this pleasant routine when the Men Dancers all joined the armed forces. In need of money, Shawn leased the property to Mary Washington Ball. The next year, Shawn leased it to ballet stars Alicia Markova and Anton Dolin, who staged an international dance festival that was so successful that a local group purchased Jacob's Pillow outright to keep the summer dance festival in operation.

Jacob's Pillow now is a dance institution, annually presenting a summer program of diverse performances. Pillow Talks are given by artists before and after events and as separate gatherings. A summer school for dancers of varying skill levels offers dance training in a wide variety of styles. For example, during the summer of 2009, Rennie Harris was an instructor. Harris is a **hip-hop** artist who has been at the forefront of turning street movement into mainstream stage art worldwide. There is a huge dance arc between 1930s ballerina Markova and twenty-first century street-based Harris.

It turned out that Jacob's Pillow, with its friendly bell clanging to announce the theater open for seating and an eclectic mix of dancers from around the world, would be the means of keeping a spark of Denishawn's fervent experimental spirit alive.

"Denishawn was preparing for their famous tour of the Orient and we were all excited. . . . I was told I looked too Oriental and would not be a true representative of Denishawn."[20] The truth lies somewhere in between. Miss Ruth never liked Graham's dancing, though Shawn encouraged her, even making her a teacher. Graham felt misunderstood and underutilized. She even carried around clippings that said Graham was the only Denishawn dancer to perform with passion and excitement. Each of this trio had a well-developed ego, and a split was inevitable.

Denishawn sputtered to an end in the early 1930s, a victim of the economic crisis of the Great Depression, as well as of the internal strains within the company. The company had accomplished great things, touring and spreading their artistic yearnings across America. Men and women began to look at stage dance as a potentially real art form, and a generation of young people was inspired to dance. By 1932, Shawn had struck off on his own, touring with his own Company of Male Dancers. He eventually turned his farm in Massachusetts, Jacob's Pillow, into an important summer dance festival. St. Denis returned to solo performances, usually in a religious setting. The couple parted, and although they never divorced, they lived separately for the rest of their long lives.

Meanwhile, on October 28, 1928, Doris Humphrey and Charles Weidman, along with 16 other dancers, made American dance history with the first performance by a modern-dance ensemble. This, in combination with Martha Graham's 1926 solo concert, established the idea of modern dance as an art form based on individual movement vocabularies unrelated to the past. Almost every modern dancer performing today can trace his or her own dance lineage back to one of these three Denishawn dancers.

Ruth St. Denis died in 1968, and Ted Shawn in 1972. No one had called their art "modern dance." After Denishawn, dancers as well as painters, musicians, and authors were called modern artists. Denishawn, in its lovely Spanish mansion overlooking Los Angeles, was the cradle of a great theater movement where dancers were taught not only how to move but also to have the confidence to assume the title of artist.

The Founding Modern-Dance Generation

I feel that the essence of dance is the expression of man—
the landscape of his soul.

—Martha Graham[21]

By the late 1920s, Americans had become accustomed to the idea of "artistic" dance. Denishawn had crisscrossed the country many times as well as making itself newsworthy with its famous Orient tour. Moreover, Isadora Duncan, although reviled in her lifetime as a decadent Communist, inspired young women across the United States to seek self-expression by putting on Greek tunics and dancing barefoot. Ballet also attracted widespread interest as Anna Pavlova toured the United States, leaving in her wake scores of would-be ballerinas, including Agnes de Mille. Meanwhile, word filtered back from Europe that Russian impressario Serge Diaghilev was presenting dazzling new productions with charismatic dancers such as Vaslav Nijinsky. The latter performed in ballets utilizing innovative collaborators, including composer Igor Stravinsky, artist Pablo Picasso, and choreographer George Balanchine.

A TIME FOR EXPERIMENTATION

This general climate of curiosity about serious dance was new. Martha Graham, Doris Humphrey, and Charles Weidman benefited from it, and were also inspired by it. The decision to leave Denishawn to evolve a personal way of moving might not have happened in a less supportive cultural climate. Each dancer had come of age professionally in the exuberant post–World War I era, when skirts went up, jazz and nightclubs thrived, movie palaces appeared across the country, and the automobile made Americans increasingly mobile. It was a time of high confidence and experimentation. Graham, Humphrey, and Weidman were uninterested in conquering Europe or in the great reforms sweeping ballet; they sought to create movement that represented American energy.

The dancers who embarked on this exciting artistic journey could not know that within a few years of their first solo concerts, this environment of high excitement and encouragement of the arts would disappear. In 1929, the crash of the stock market precipitated a worldwide economic depression. Breadlines, hobos, and striking workers replaced the high-living flappers and their tuxedoed admirers. "Brother, Can You Spare a Dime?" was the song on everyone's lips. Abroad, Adolf Hitler seized power in Germany, as did Benito Mussolini in Italy, and civil war broke out in Spain. The confident, affluent 1920s disappeared into the fearful, impoverished Depression era of the 1930s. Inevitably, the change was reflected in the arts.

Martha Graham did not immediately take to the stage and become the great lady of American modern dance. She had a long period of trial and error before entering her great era of sustained choreographic invention in her 40s. When she first left Denishawn, she happily performed for two years in the Greenwich Village Follies, becoming something of a Broadway star where "each night one of my solos," she exulted, "would stop the show."[22] Later, restless and unsatisfied with the life of a showgirl, even a very popular one, Graham left the Follies in 1925 in order, as she stated, "to create my own dances, on my own body."

Although Graham remained a loner all her life, she had a knack for finding people who saw something special in her and were willing to lend her substantial assistance. This happened when she had first applied at Denishawn and been turned away by Miss Ruth, only to have

In the mid-1920s, Martha Graham set out to create her own dances based on the principles of muscle contraction and release. Here, Graham poses in a scene from the dance *Salem Shore*, circa 1943.

Ted Shawn step in. He recognized Graham's sheer determination and decided to encourage her desire to become a better dancer. Although the relationship between Shawn and Graham ended in disillusionment, each acknowledged the role Shawn had played in Martha's Denishawn career. Shawn went so far as to say, "I trained her. Ruth didn't and wouldn't. There'd be no Martha Graham without me."[23] Graham, however, had a different take on her Denishawn experience, saying, "I worshipped everything about Miss Ruth—how she walked, how she danced. Miss Ruth was everything to me, but I got stuck with Ted who really was something of a dud."[24]

Her Broadway exit came about when Rouben Mamoulian, a Russian-born theatrical director, invited her to act as codirector of the newly established dance department at the Eastman School of Music in Rochester, New York. George Eastman, whose invention of the Kodak camera in 1888 had made him wealthy enough to turn to philanthropy, had brought in Mamoulian to direct his school of music. Mamoulian surprised everyone by insisting on including a dance department. "Dance," he declared, "is the foundation of the theater."[25] Mamoulian had seen Graham perform on Broadway and thought her a gifted dancer with an unusual personality—and, like himself, a very idiosyncratic talent.

Louis Horst, who had spent time in Vienna after leaving Denishawn as its musical director, joined Graham at Eastman. Others would regard such artistic encouragement and collaboration as wonderful, but Graham, who did not have a spirit suited to working at institutions—with or without congenial colleagues—left after one year.

Using three Eastman students, Graham gave her first independent dance concert in New York City at the Forty-Eighth Street Theater on April 18, 1926—but it was not the debut that would have critics hailing her as a genius. Alas, even some of the titles of these first dances show that she was still locked into a Denishawn approach to movement and programming: *Three Gopi Maidens*, *Florentine Madonna*, and *Clair de Lune*. Any of these would have been appropriate for one of Miss Ruth's dance dramas or music visualizations. The newspapers remarked that the work was merely "pretty" and "graceful,"[26] and Graham herself conceded her first dances were "influenced by Denishawn."[27]

Graham continued to experiment with movement, focusing on a new way for the dancer to breathe that she called "a contraction and a release" (also known as **contraction-release**)—that is, not only to breathe involuntarily, but also to exaggerate the sharp intake of breath and its explosive expulsion. Even today, when a Graham-trained dancer performs this torso-based movement, the viewer can see the body pull back at its center and then expand outward—like being socked in the stomach. Graham based her dances not on simple counts, as most choreographers do, but on breath counts: short, fast breath quickly expelled for anger, and longer, slower breath counts for quieter moods. Used this way, she invited the audience, instinctively breathing the same rhythm, to be pulled emotionally into the performance as well.[28]

Most stage-dance techniques before Graham elongated the body and moved it upward into space, as did ballet. Graham, on the other hand, celebrated the floor and the earth—sitting on it, falling on it, and touching it. Deliberately violating ballet's classical technique of pointing the foot and creating a line of the leg from thigh to toe, she danced flat-footed and with bare (and often flexed) feet. These innovations were not new—they had all been employed at Denishawn—but that company used them in the service of exoticism. Graham used these techniques without glamorous trappings. She did not disguise the effort that went into her movements—she sweated. She would not leap; she pounced. When she kicked her leg in the air, the audience saw a dirty foot. It was not pretty, as Graham acknowledged: "In many ways I showed onstage what most people came to the theater to avoid."[29]

It would take years for Martha Graham's technique to mature, but all the elements were in place by the late 1920s and early 1930s. In 1927, she presented a solo dance called *Revolt*, which was about man's injustice to man. It was definitely not a Denishawn or ballet topic. Reviewers called this work "stark" and even "ugly." Graham had found her idiom, and from this point on, she experimented with movement that made a statement. She wanted technique to service her ideas rather than demonstrate dance virtuosity. It was not that she deliberately wanted to antagonize audiences, "but I'd rather they disliked me than be apathetic, because that is the kiss of death," observed Graham.[30]

In 1929, she presented *Heretic*, her first concert dance for a company of dancers. Wearing a simple long, white jersey dress, Graham confronted 12 women in identical long, black dresses who became, in her words, "a wall of defiance that I could not break."[31] A Breton song played and then stopped; at this moment of silence, the women in black reformed into another group. Explained Graham, "I was the heretic desperately trying to force myself free of the darkness of my oppressors."[32] She herself was a heretic in the world of dance, challenging old conceptions of dance and facing similar opposition. People either loved her boldness or hated it.

The next year, she created and performed *Lamentation*, a solo performed seated while she stretched and moved inside a long tube of jersey material— ". . . to indicate," Graham said, "the tragedy that obsesses the body, the ability to stretch inside your own skin, to witness and test the perimeter and boundaries of grief. . . ."[33] Martha Graham had found her genius.

BREAKING AWAY FROM THE SHADOW OF DENISHAWN

Martha Graham was not the only former Denishawn dancer performing new work on the concert stage. Doris Humphrey and Charles Weidman left Denishawn far less dramatically than Graham. From the beginning, their company, known as Humphrey-Weidman, was composed of both men and women; Graham's company, in contrast, was all-female for its first 15 years. Although both Humphrey and Weidman were powerful soloists, their work was conceived primarily for a group to perform. Humphrey was an exquisite dancer performing "like a nymph" in airy, light, delicate movements, in direct contrast to Graham's earthbound fierceness.[34] Weidman was that rare performer in modern dance—a humorist and mime, someone whose most celebrated dances made people laugh. Neither had the immense personality of Graham, her glamour, nor her occasionally irritating high-handedness.

Humphrey had come to Denishawn after teaching dance in Chicago, and it was St. Denis who saw her talent and urged her to perform. To the end of her days, Humphrey remained at heart a natural teacher, leaving behind a legacy of talented dancers. One of these, José Limón, would be at the forefront of the next modern-dance generation. She never was interested solely in creating new dances; she was equally committed to developing a dance language that facilitated movement composition.

If Martha Graham wanted to explore her interior life, Doris Humphrey was much more interested in abstract questions about the nature of movement. "My entire technique," said Humphrey, "consists of the development of the process of falling away from and returning to equilibrium."[35] In the danger of the fall and the peace of recovery, Humphrey saw the quest for adventure and the desire for peace. She described the movement between the two actions as the "arc between two deaths."[36] She insisted that one did not "make up" dances, but rather that one composed them. This view influenced every serious dance artist who came in contact with her.

Doris Humphrey was considered Martha Graham's equal, and even to this day, some believe Humphrey was the greater artist of modern dance's founding trio because of the methodology she set in place to compose dance. This is an old argument not dissimilar to the equally fierce and forgotten battles between supporters of modern dance and ballet.

Martha Graham performed in one way or another until she died in 1991 at age 97. She had appeared on stage, in film, and in television. She had taught dancers, written books, given lectures, and graciously accepted awards from everyone from presidents of the United States to university presidents. By sheer force of will, she had turned herself into a beauty—a mesmerizing presence both onstage and off.

By contrast, Doris Humphrey was a red-haired, pale-skinned, and fragile, fine-boned woman of real beauty and an unassuming nature. By 1944, she had given up performing because of severe arthritis but continued working as an artistic director, choreographer, and teacher for José Limón, the most talented of the Humphrey-Weidman dancers. She died in 1958, revered by students and audiences alike. She was not well known to the world at large and performed too early to be enveloped in the celebrity machine that caught up with some of the early surviving modern-dance pioneers later in the century. Agnes de Mille said of Humphrey, "She cared far less about production, little about recognition, and nothing at all about remuneration. In this, I believe, she was unique, being compelled to create for the joy of the work to the very end of her life."[37]

One of the bylaws of dance—whether ballet or modern—is that movement should respond to music. Boldly, Humphrey composed completely abstract dances to be performed in silence, an idea that is still considered very avant-garde. An early Humphrey solo, 1929's *Life of the Bee*, had her dancing to the sound of someone blowing on a tissue-covered comb mimicking the sound of a bee. In 1931, Humphrey created what is still considered one of her major works: *The Shakers*, a

Doris Humphrey, pictured during a performance in Seattle, Washington, in 1925, was considered every bit as talented as her contemporary Martha Graham. Like Graham, Humphrey was a member of Denishawn but left the group in 1928 to form her own company with Charles Weidman.

dance for seven people that centered on Humphrey's solo in which "with wide skirts swirling about her, Doris Humphrey lifted her arms, opened her hands, and raised a transfigured face. To the music of a drum, an accordion, and a wordless soprano voice, Humphrey and her dancers re-created a moment in the past for American theater."[38]

Her partner, Charles Weidman, had simply shown up at Denishawn one day after having seen the company perform in his native Nebraska. He had been an artistically inclined child and was headed toward a career in architecture. "Then," he observed later, "Ruth St. Denis came to the Orpheum Theatre in Lincoln, with her pageant of India, Egypt, and Greece, and there was my history of dancing before me. I just put two and two together, and from then on I wanted to do that kind of dancing."[39] Shawn gave him a couple months of instruction and then sent him on the road. Weidman survived his sink-or-swim introduction to performance and went on to create dances himself during the Denishawn years. Shawn capitalized on Weidman's gifts as a mime, creating amusing dances such as *Danse Americaine* for the Denishawn repertory. In 1925, Weidman described how this dance was to be performed: "The character is a small mill-town dude. He is the sport of the town and knows it. He is afraid of nothing on earth but the 'skoits'! Remember to keep this spirit of bravado throughout the entire dance. There are no regular fixed steps: It is merely the interpretation of a story by gesture."[40]

Weidman was as involved as Humphrey in creating the technique that came to be associated with the Humphrey-Weidman troupe, but balanced out her cerebral and refined approach with his satirical gifts. If Humphrey was drawn to the logical, Weidman was drawn to the illogical. He liked to draw a movement from an everyday incident and then use it in a situation removed from the context in which it had occurred. Much of his work was shaped by his own skill as a brilliant mime and comic and by his talent for finding the telling gesture.

These young experimenters set out not only to create new work, but also to find an audience. They were forced to consider the very problems that had plagued Denishawn: how to support themselves and their dancers while continuing to create and perform. No one wanted to go into Broadway revues again, nor did they want to tour. Teaching classes in their studios helped some but not much. The costs of renting a theater or mounting a production were beyond most of their means. Until they could find a way to financially survive, their artistic endeavors were simply marking time.

In 1929, the Dance Repertory Theater was formed to pool resources and engage a single manager, share advertising costs, and even rent a theater for as long as a week. The organizing group consisted of Martha Graham, Doris Humphrey, Charles Weidman, and Helen Tamiris, who had actually suggested this approach. The idea was to find a way to ensure both financial support and an audience, thereby addressing the most serious problems facing these dancer/choreographers' futures.

This effort was doomed from the start. None of the big three—Graham, Humphrey, or Weidman—considered Tamiris to be an artist on their level. Humphrey and Weidman worried about being "organized to death" as they had been in Denishawn. And Humphrey thought Graham was "a snake."[41] For her part, Graham hated collaboration of any kind, as she was always an intensely single-focused and independent personality. When José Limón stood in the wings watching her dance, she asked the stage manager to tell him she "would not tolerate being watched from the wing."[42]

The Dance Repertory Theater experiment only lasted two seasons. This left Graham, Humphrey, and Weidman right where they had been before: trying to create new dance and get it on stage while somehow supporting themselves financially. Their work, however, had not gone unnoticed.

A young educator named Martha Hill had been "fairly hypnotized" by seeing Graham dance and even briefly became a Graham dancer before turning back to education.[43] Hill became a pioneer in advancing the cause of dance in colleges and universities, beginning first at New York University and then at Midwestern colleges. But it would be Bennington College that would become the place where modern dance would find a secure base.

In 1932, Bennington College was founded in southern Vermont to establish an avant-garde educational program. Martha Hill originated its dance program and received permission to establish summer sessions that would bring in the great modern dance leaders. Not only would they teach, but they would also create their own dances and perform locally. Nearby, Ted Shawn's Massachusetts farm, Jacob's Pillow, opened in 1933 as a summer festival, primarily showcasing his Male Dancers troupe. When both Bennington College and the Jacob's Pillow Festival were up and running, the area became the focus of avant-garde dance. Word spread throughout the nation, although the Bennington group looked down on Shawn's work as reactionary and old-fashioned.

German dancer and choreographer Mary Wigman was influenced by the same movement and emotion theories that served to inspire Isadora Duncan. Unlike Duncan, however, Wigman was not afraid to explore the ugliness that can be tied to human emotions and relationships in her dance.

The Bennington program got underway in 1934 with a faculty consisting of Graham, Humphrey, Weidman, and newcomer Hanya Holm. Bringing these maverick experimental dancers into the college curriculum supported the artists in ways beyond their wildest dreams. It was the Great Depression, yet here they were with free theaters, studios, and production workshops. They had freedom to work, students to teach, theaters to perform in, audiences to see the work—and prestige.

Hanya Holm, the new name among the experimenters, was actually German. She had come to the United States in 1931 to set up a dance studio teaching the technique of fellow German Mary Wigman. Germany was the only country other than the United States to develop modern dance early in the century. Wigman was an important innovator, influenced by the same movement and theories on expressing emotion that had inspired Isadora Duncan. Yet, unlike her contemporary Duncan, Wigman was not afraid of being ugly or exploring unattractive subjects. Her work has been associated with the emotional excesses and high drama of German Expressionist art.

When Holm arrived in New York to set up a Mary Wigman school, she found that her American students were not naturally suited to the German Expressionist approach, with its distortion and heightened theatricality. Wigman gave Holm permission to change her school's American curriculum to make it more suited to American temperament and skills. Had Mary Wigman not been persecuted by the Nazis and forced to close all her dance schools, the history of modern dance might have become a joint American and German story. Instead, German Expressionist modern dance as taught by Holm at Bennington and at her studio was folded into the story of the first pioneers of American modern dance, and did not become an independent component of a worldwide explosion of new movement. By the time Wigman began to perform and teach once more after World War II, Graham, Humphrey, and Weidman were celebrated artists, and Wigman, major innovator that she was, remained merely an important footnote to the main story.

Modern dance had come into its own by the 1940s. No longer a dancer's solitary vision or a choreographer's experiment, modern dance existed as a theater art. Soon, the burgeoning art form would experience a new generation of rebels, as well as contact with other dance genres.

The Reformers and Post-Modern Dance

. . . dancing is a spiritual exercise in physical form, and . . . what is seen is what it is.

—Merce Cunningham[44]

On the small stage of the Coolidge Theatre at the Library of Congress in Washington, D.C., Martha Graham stood taking a bow. It was October 30, 1944, and, at age 50, she had just danced the lead role of a young bride in the premiere of her *Appalachian Spring*. The radiant Graham accepted the applause hand-in-hand with Erick Hawkins, a 35-year-old dancer who had appeared in the stage role of her bridegroom—a role he would play later in real life. Merce Cunningham, a phenomenally talented dancer who had portrayed the frontier preacher, was on her other side. It was Graham who—with funds from the Coolidge Foundation (headed by music patron Elizabeth Sprague Coolidge)—had commissioned composer Aaron Copeland to create the ballet's original score. Her act marked the first time a major commission would be given to a modern-dance choreographer, and the performance piece would become the most famous of all Graham's dances. Furthermore, Copland's score, based on a Shaker hymn theme, would go on to win a Pulitzer Prize. *Appalachian Spring* made it absolutely clear to the world at large that modern dance was no longer to be considered a vaudeville novelty. It had come of age as an art form.

Shown here in 1944 at the age of 50, Martha Graham (*left*) played a featured role in the ballet *Appalachian Spring*. The original ballet is preserved on film, produced for a 1958 public television performance. In it, the 64-year-old Graham performs on designer Isamu Noguchi's minimalist prairie set.

A NEW GENERATION TAKES THE STAGE

Yet, within a few years of the *Appalachian Spring* premiere, the trio of dancer/choreographers (Martha Graham, Doris Humphrey, and Charles Weidman) largely responsible for this remarkable theatrical accomplishment would find themselves considered out-of-date. Young dancers, many of them students of these modern-dance pioneers, began to look for new subjects to draw upon as they explored ideas of how to artistically move bodies in different ways. The "historic" first modern-dance generation wanted to establish itself as uniquely American, taking its subjects from the social and intellectual concerns of the era. Above all, these individuals wanted to be taken seriously and to erase lingering associations of experimental dance with vaudeville and show business.

If modern-dance innovators shared any single view, it was that they were not doing ballet. They wanted to move freely. From their vantage point, these groundbreakers saw ballet dancers as trapped in an established movement system based on fixed positions of the body, feet and arms, and ballet as a performing style that had been codified centuries earlier. Every generation of ballet choreographers and dancers gave ballet a new look, but it was true that they did not change the basic steps and positions. The moderns could not see the way ballet had changed and how it too was in the process of a movement revolution—what the innovators saw was stagnation. Modern-dance choreographers wanted to create new ways of moving suited to their own, more democratic time; they rejected movements they saw as tied to an aristocratic past.

The disdain modern dancers shared for ballet was returned in full measure. Ballet performers and audiences alike thought all the moderns' grand, mythic statements and high-purposed intentions were simply smoke screens covering up the latters' inability to dance.

Many of the earliest innovators of modern dance were women, but this, too, was about to change. Dancers from Isadora Duncan to Martha Graham had had the extra burden of proving that a woman could construct a dance that was not about the shape of her legs, but about the content of her mind and spirit. No one had questioned whether or not a woman should dance. The apparent sexism reflected as much as anything the lack of esteem that dance was given as a theater art.

The modern-dance revolution did not happen immediately. Martha Graham did not retire from performing until 1969, when she was 75 years old. Even then, she stayed on stage, usually sitting in a chair and wearing flowing garments as she introduced her company's performance. Doris Humphrey, however, retired from performing in 1945. She had struggled for years with near-crippling arthritis and, finally, as her hip pain became unbearable, was forced to stop performing. Still, Humphrey did not stop working with dance, although her retirement did bring to an end the Humphrey-Weidman Group.

The troupe's most talented dancer, José Limón, went on to found an experimental company of his own in 1946. The Mexican-born Limón, a dancer/choreographer of great presence, took the unique step of asking Doris Humphrey if she would act as an artistic director along with himself. By doing this, Limón ensured the continuation of Humphrey's dance theories and dance works, as he incorporated Humphrey's dances into the repertoire of his newly emerging troupe. The José Limón Dance Company still exists, although its founder died in 1972. It still performs Doris Humphrey's work along with Limón's in an unbroken line that exists nowhere else in modern dance.

Charles Weidman established a studio and a small company of his own at the time Humphrey-Weidman dissolved. He was still living in a room off his rehearsal space and giving Sunday afternoon dance programs when he died in 1975. One of Weidman's most famous students was Bob Fosse, the choreographer who took Weidman's wit and humor and added the sharp edge of jazz dance to became one of America's most important Broadway and Hollywood choreographers, staging such works as *Chicago* and the movie version of *Cabaret*.

Although Graham, Humphrey, and Weidman are the recognized pioneers responsible for founding modern dance, they were not the only modern dancers working in the 1930s and into the 1940s. As previously discussed, among their contemporaries, Helen Tamaris had organized the Dance Repertory Theatre experiment, and Hanya Holm was an important instructor at the Bennington College Dance Festival. Both women created serious dances reflecting the social concerns of their

One of the Humphrey-Weidman troupe's most talented dancers was Mexican-born José Limón, who moved to New York City in 1928. Limón (*left*), pictured leaping in mid-air with Charles Weidman in 1939, would go on to form his own dance group, the José Limón Dance Company, in 1946.

times. Ironically, however, both Tamaris and Holm, as well as Fosse, would find their lasting fame choreographing for Broadway.

Tamiris is particularly remembered as one of the first dancer/choreographers to turn to African-American material, and her *Negro Spirituals* is still considered an innovation. This was not one dance but a series created through the years 1929 to 1942 using African-American themes and music. The Federal Dance Project, organized in 1935 by the Works Progress Administration as part of the effort to combat the devastating unemployment caused by the Great Depression, funded Tamiris's *How Long Brethren?* in 1937. It was the first dance in the United States to be created with public funding. Yet, Tamaris is chiefly remembered today as a Tony award–winning choreographer for the musical *Touch and Go* and even more so for her work in *Annie Get Your Gun.*

Holm remained an important teacher as well as choreographer, and 1937's *Trend*, which she composed while in charge of the workshop group at Bennington College, had the very topical theme of a society being destroyed by false values. In 1941 she established a summer dance institute at Colorado College in Colorado Springs, and she left a legacy of many outstanding students, including Alwin Nikolais, whose work would relight the flame of German Expressionism in American modern dance. Holm, too, found her greatest recognition on Broadway as choreographer for *Kiss Me Kate* (for which she received the New York Drama Critics Award), *My Fair Lady*, and *Camelot*.

Black dance was more than an occasional theme for modern dance, however—it was a thriving dance category of its own. Katherine Dunham and Pearl Primus, two black women who both held doctorates in anthropology, were presenting the genuine article—based on field research they had undertaken in Africa and the Caribbean—to wildly enthusiastic audiences of every color. Dunham's first important work, *L'Ag'ya*, also supported by the Federal Dance Project, depicted life on Martinique, and she typically presented exciting and glamorous movement and dazzling costumes representing black culture. Primus did this as well, but also focused on grimmer visions of African-American life. These two women anthropologist-performers brought black movement out of the specialty revue or nightclub to the concert stage.

In Los Angeles, Lester Horton—a man with wide-ranging interests in dance experimentation and a particular fascination with Native American culture—formed a dance company in 1932. Horton developed his own technique that centered on an unmoving torso with asymmetrical movements of the arms and legs. (Horton's most important student, Alvin Ailey, made this style his own. In dance after dance, Ailey's troupe drew together and leaned their torsos into space, centered and still, while bent-elbowed arms moved in the air like wings, suggesting flight or escape.) Through the years Horton had tried everything from designing outdoor pageants to choreographing nightclub acts and working on movie musicals. He established the first theater in the United States devoted solely to dance. His most important legacy, however, was that his dance company was the first fully integrated company in the United States, drawing on African-American, Mexican-American, Japanese, and white dancers. Horton dancers, Alvin Ailey being foremost, carried more than good dancing into the next generation; they brought a color-blind eye to what they did and who did it.

In Martha Graham's company, an extremely talented male dancer, Merce Cunningham, had been singled out repeatedly for praise, particularly for his role as the preacher in *Appalachian Spring* and for his fantastic high leaps as March in Graham's ode to Emily Dickinson, *Letter to the World*. While still dancing with Graham, Cunningham began working in creative partnership with avant-garde composer John Cage, whom he had met in Seattle during his dance student years. When not dancing character roles with Graham, he was experimenting with movement that would be only about dancing. The first joint performance by Cunningham and Cage was given at the Humphrey-Weidman Studio on 16th Street in 1944. *New York Herald Tribune* critic Edwin Denby said of this performance, "I have never seen a first recital that combined such taste, such technical finish, such originality of dance material"; he added that the effect of hearing Cage's "odd timbres" with Cunningham's "dancing has an effect of extreme elegance in isolation."[45]

Born in 1919 and still working up until the time he died in July 2009, Cunningham never stopped devising movement that derived its value from what is done in the moment, at a particular performance. His dances had no subject, and no historical, biographical, or psychological meaning. The dance simply exists. That does not mean, however, that he created simple dances. His interest in both chance and indeterminacy led to complex dance compositions. He used chance to decide, often by a flip of a coin or drawing a number, which movement sequence would follow which and who would dance it. The elements thus came together at the performance. It was not the same thing as improvisation, because each movement phrase had been set by the choreographer. Since their order was undetermined until the actual performance, they had to be able to fit together once the cards were thrown into the air. It was like creating a puzzle in which every piece must fit but which was never assembled in the same way.

At age 90, Merce Cunningham was still throwing everything up in the air by making new dance compositions and leading company class. To celebrate the occasion of his 90th birthday, on April 16, 2009, Cunningham premiered a full evening composition entitled *Nearly Ninety*. Performed at Brooklyn Academy of Music, this work was created in

Merce Cunningham won acclaim for his role as the preacher in *Appalachian Spring*, but he would go on to become one of the most influential choreographers in modern dance during a career that spanned more than 50 years. Cunningham is pictured here at the premiere of *Appalachian Spring* in 1944.

collaboration with the legendary indie rock group Sonic Youth, former Led Zeppelin bassist John Paul Jones, and mixed-media sound composer Takehisa Kosugi.

Dance critic Joan Acocella wrote in *The New Yorker* about the event:

> For his anti-classicism and his anti-lyricism, together with his more ingratiating qualities, notably the cleanness and intensity of his

dances, he will always be recognized as the foremost representative of high modernism—the Joyce-Pound-Beckett kind—in the history of modern dance, and as a creator of beauty and meaning on their level. On opening night, there was a little ceremony after the show, and Cunningham came out onstage in a wheelchair, wearing a black velvet jacket, black sneakers, and an embarrassed smile.[46]

Completely comfortable with twenty-first century technology, Cunningham decided the best way to reach young dancers worldwide was to put his company class online. This gave anyone with access to a computer the opportunity to see and take class with one of the greatest of modern-dance masters. They could see his teaching technique and learn from his instruction. Cunningham acknowledged his age by sitting down to give instruction but knew exactly what and how he wanted his company to move. "Curve and tilt," he instructed, "but not fast," he corrected them.

Cunningham was still Cunningham. There is no one point of reference in a Cunningham dance—no central couple, no corps, and no repeating movement patterns to guide the viewer's eye. Even the center of the stage is not necessarily the focus of attention. John Cage's music is created on its own without reference to anything the choreographer is doing, as are the sets and costumes designed by important visual artists. This is as close to total abstraction as anyone has ever come in sustained movement.

The dances Cunningham created had no inherent dramatic value. They exist as movement and tend to either fascinate or repel by that element alone. In the 1950s at the height of Abstract Expressionism, with Jackson Pollock painting by dribbling color onto a canvas, Cunningham essentially did the same thing by mixing his dance elements somewhat by chance at the performance moment. This was—and is—so radical and demanding that audiences routinely walk out of his performances, and more than 50 years later, his are regarded as the most avant-garde work. Ironically, Cunningham died only three months after his triumph with *Nearly Ninety*. Seemingly, this was how this great dance figure would have wanted to leave the world stage.

Cunningham's contemporary Alwin Nikolais had been a Bennington dance student who had gone on to become Hanya Holm's assistant before devising his own dance abstractions. Nikolais experimented with lights, color, and costumes to transform the entire stage space into moving abstractions that engulfed the dancers. He called what he did "dance theater," although none of his dances had a plot. In his high theatricality, he demonstrated his lineage through Holm to German Expressionist dance and its great figure Mary Wigman, who had used masks and wigs to distort her appearance. Nikolais, in fact, had become interested in going into dance when he saw Mary Wigman perform in one of her three tours of the United States in the early 1930s. His choreographic work was like a painting creating itself in front of the audience's eyes. Anonymous dancers stretched inside jersey tubes or between elastic tapes while colors changed and light shifted in focus and intensity. Everything on stage—the movements, costumes, and music—all came out of Nikolais's imagination.

Nikolais's 1953 work *Masks, Props, and Mobiles* was not even considered by many critics to be a dance at all, because all the performers wore costumes that disguised or hid their bodies. In one section, they were enclosed in cloth bags that they moved and manipulated from within, creating what looked like kinetic sculpture pieces. Because Nikolais so often made what were called "dances of sorcery or carnival in which the dancers may be engulfed by an entranced landscape light . . . disappear, metamorphose, be imprinted with whirling patterns," critics often did not know quite what to make of what he was doing. Nikolais was not interested in developing dances exploring the human psyche; he wanted to help both dancers and the audience look beyond the personal, saying, "I wanted man to identify with things other than himself."[47]

Choreographer Paul Taylor is an important transitional figure between the modern-dance pioneers and the free-floating world of modern dance today. Taylor trained at Juilliard and the Martha Graham School in New York while assisting artist Robert Rauschenberg and decorating store windows at night. He danced in Merce Cunningham's troupe before moving on to Martha Graham's company, of which he was a member for seven years. In his real job, Taylor was partnering Graham herself, who was still dancing in her sixties, in her highly dramatic *Clytemnestra* or in roles that required a more imposing stature, such as that of Hercules in *Alcestis*. But on his own, Taylor was making a name for himself as someone at the forefront of a very different kind of dance.

Taylor was experimenting with movement that had absolutely nothing to do with Greek myths, as Graham sometimes did. He was interested in the way people walked, sat, and ran—in other words, the most ordinary movements of everyday life. Thus, he began exploring movement without using set dance steps. He expanded the idea and thought that if dance could be broadened to include everyday moves, perhaps its accompaniment could, too.

Taylor used studio showcases to try out ideas, including *Duet*, in which neither he nor his accompanist moved for the duration of John Cage's *Non Score*. In the same showcase, Taylor—wearing a business suit

Paul Taylor performed in the companies of Martha Graham and Merce Cunningham and went on to form his own dance group, the Paul Taylor Dance Company, in 1954. Taylor is pictured with Bettie De Jong and Renee Kimball in 1964.

and carrying a briefcase—walked back and forth across the stage as the sound of a telephone's recorded time announcement played in a piece called *Epic*. Proto-Pop artist Robert Rauschenberg designed the set for this piece. Louis Horst, long Graham's musical associate and an important composer in his own right, reviewed Taylor's *Seven New Dances* (which included *Duet and Epic*) for *Dance Observer* with four inches of blank space and his initials "L.H." neatly printed at the bottom. Martha Graham shook her finger at Taylor and called him a "naughty boy."[48]

Eventually, Taylor learned to trust his own instinctive love of movement, going from anti-dance and avant-garde to creating plotless dances of great joyous—and even athletic—movement performed to classical and popular music. As a dancer/choreographer, he did not become frozen in the experiments of one era, although he did occasionally slip some of his earlier experimental ideas into his later work. Twenty years after his *Epic* exploration, Taylor's 1975 work *Esplanade* sent his company walking, running, jumping, sliding, and repeatedly falling to Bach in a glorious burst of lyric dance where ordinary movement became balletic. No one walked out of that performance, and critics described the beauty of merging these unlikely movements with such sublime music.

THE POST-MODERN DANCE GENERATION

During the 1960s, the United States lurched from one internal upheaval to another, beginning with the assassination of President John F. Kennedy. An escalating Vietnam War and universal draft provoked anti-war activities across the country. At the same time, the civil rights movement exploded under the leadership of Dr. Martin Luther King with sit-ins, marches, and campaigns for voting rights. When Dr. King Jr. was assassinated in 1968, riots erupted. Yet, unlike the 1930s and 1940s, when social upheaval inspired the arts and shaped the look of modern dance, the sheer violence and personal disaffection of the 1960s seemed to push artists away from examining these massive problems and further into abstraction.

The new choreographers of the 1960s were inspired by Cunningham, Taylor, and Nikolais, but they went further than these men. They wanted to be as abstract as Cunningham without his complex organization, to push Taylor's experiments with ordinary movement as far as they could go, and to depersonalize their work without using masks or costumes. The Judson Dance Theatre—or Judson Group, as this loose collection of dancers was known—got its name almost 15 years after they had been presenting individual movement experimentation at the Judson Memorial Church on Washington Square in Greenwich Village.

Judson Dance was never a self-conscious movement. People came and went throughout the 1960s, using the studio space at the church, watching each other's work, and taking lessons in dance composition at the Cunningham studio. There were no dues, no rules, and no organization, but there was a manifesto. At one time or another during that decade, it included Trisha Brown, Lucinda Childs, Laura Dean, Simone Forti, Meredith Monk, and Twyla Tharp. These dancers were all young, talented, and eager to see if walking, running, or even falling might be dance. Did a dance have to happen on a stage? What if a musician danced? The Judson manifesto, created by dancer Yvonne Rainer, stated:

> No to spectacle, no to virtuosity, no to transformations and magic and make-believe, no to glamour and transcendency of the star image, no to the heroic, no to the anti-heroic, no to trash imagery, no to involvement of performer or spectator, no to style, no to camp, no to seductions of spectator by the wiles of the performer, no to eccentricity, no to moving or being moved.

These young experimenters were uninterested in historic modern dance with its allusions to myth and psychology. Equally, they dismissed ballet, considering its classical technique to be constraining. They tested the very notion of theatrical dance with pieces such as Trisha Brown's 1971 *Roof Piece*, in which dancers stationed on rooftops relayed movements that were passed along from rooftop to rooftop while observers stood on sidewalks far below. David Gordon dropped his trousers and spat during his 1966 solo work *Walks and Digressions* and was roundly booed. Audiences regularly walked out on Judson Church performances, but others took their place. In a continuing series of work, Gordon explored chairs—he sat on them, he fell off them, he tipped them over, and tried just about anything imaginable with a chair. He maddened people, but he challenged and ignited their imaginations as well.

TRISHA BROWN: THE LONGEVITY OF JUDSON DANCE THEATER

On May 9, 2009, Trisha Brown, one of the key figures of the Judson Dance Theater movement, had a major opening in New York City. This time the opening was a show of her visual art at the Chelsea gallery Sikkema Jenkins & Co. Through the years this major modern-dance figure had often shown drawings and sketches in group exhibitions. This, however, was her first major solo show. As a choreographer, she often collaborated with avant-garde artist Robert Rauschenberg, whose creations resonated with her own abstract movement experimentation. As a working method for her choreography, Brown preferred to get on her hands and knees and sketch the lines and placement of the dancers. "Dancers think like this," she told *The New York Times*. "I don't think people do."

In her seventies, Brown began to pull back from the rigorous physical activity, although she did not stop working. Occasionally, she performs with her nine-member dance troupe. Increasingly, she seems content to direct her dancers while continuing her own personal exploration of the visual arts. She remains committed to choreography based on ordinary movement and the element of surprise. At a recent gallery performance entitled *So the Audience Does Not Know Whether I Have Stopped Dancing*, Brown positioned live dancers on the gallery walls

These dancers became the first of the **Post-Modern** dance generation. Historic modern dance no longer looked new—its movement solutions were dated. Worse, many of the early experimenters had created

and asked visitors to lie on the gallery floor and contemplate the ceiling.

This is the same experimenter who in the 1970s designed a series she called "equipment pieces." *Walking on the Wall* presented dancers literally walking down vertical walls using ropes, pulleys, and mountain climbing gear for support. Brown also created a solo called *Man Walking Down the Side of a Building.* Terrifying to watch, yet constructed to be safe, the solo was typical of Brown's innovative ways of transforming dance. She constructed a series of dances based on mathematical systems of accumulation. *Primary Accumulation*, choreographed in 1972, consists of 30 movements accumulated thus: 1; 1.2; 1.2.3; 1.2.3.4 and on to the full count.

In her ability to keep creatively active, Brown reflects the astounding endurance of the Judson School. For example, Twyla Tharp choreographed two Broadway musicals, including 2002's *Movin' Out*. This enormous hit used Billy Joel's music and is still being presented across the country. Other Judson dancers have remained active in a variety of ways. David Gordon is a member of Actor's Studio and has worked as a theatrical director at the Guthrie Theater in Minneapolis, the American Repertory Theater in Cambridge, Massachusetts, and other regional companies. Lucinda Childs directed the opera *Zaide* at the opera house in Brussels, Belgium. Tharp and Brown have also choreographed and staged operas. In their youth, these dance artists changed the way we think about stage movement, and they are still finding new ways to push the artistic envelope.

techniques full of rules and requirements almost as severe as those of ballet. Because of what happened at Judson Church, Post-Modern dancers today feel free to move in any way they choose, wear whatever they prefer, move with or without music, and collaborate with anyone—from painters to videographers. The high theatricality of Alwin Nikolais merged into the intense and intellectually demanding experiments of Merce Cunningham, and were then transformed by the ordinary moves Paul Taylor explored into dance of unlimited possibility.

While the Post-Modern movement was underway, another dance revolution was taking place. Alvin Ailey had formed an African-American modern dance troupe in the early 1950s after the death of his mentor, Lester Horton. Ailey not only sought to showcase his own choreography but also to provide creative employment for African-American dancers and choreographers. He wanted to reveal and celebrate the black experience in America. This was not anthropological re-creation of traditional

In 1958, Alvin Ailey formed the Alvin Ailey American Dance Theater in New York City. The group opened up opportunities for African-American dancers to perform modern dance but also served to promote the black experience in America. Here, members of the Alvin Ailey American Dance Theater rehearse a scene in *Revelations*, Ailey's most famous work.

black dance or even theatrical versions of them. Instead, this would be modern dance in the purest, historic sense of using movement to portray ideas and social viewpoints on the concert stage.

In 1960, Ailey premiered what would become his company's best-known work, *Revelations*, in which dancers performed to black spirituals. Ailey's masterpiece manages to be both a statement about oppression and yet an explosion of joy. It was the right dance for the right time. As his proud dancers, parasols lifted over their heads, went "Wading in the Water," they permanently took their place in the history of dance. Throughout the 1960s, audiences stood with tears in their eyes, black and white alike, to applaud this pure expression of the hunger of the era to face down and destroy the evils of segregation and bigotry.

The battle to establish modern dance as an American art form was over. Modern dance was acknowledged, and its choreographers became cultural heroes. Martha Graham, for one, received a Presidential Medal of Freedom. Merce Cunningham was awarded a National Medal of Arts, and France gave him the Legion d'Honneur. There really was only one last wall to be brought down—that between modern dance and ballet.

Fusion

How do you make a dance? My answer is simple. "Put yourself in motion."

—Twyla Tharp[49]

It was the first time that ballet and modern dance were presented on the same stage. The year was 1959, and ballet's great twentieth-century innovator, George Balanchine, artistic director and founding genius of New York City Ballet, reached a hand across the divide between classical ballet and modern dance. He invited Martha Graham to cochoreograph a two-part work called *Episodes* with him. Using the same music, they would each choreograph a dance. The two dances would give the audience a glimpse of how two artists working in different dance traditions used the same music, and how these results would look danced one after the other. It was not a contest or even a challenge, but an opportunity for the choreographers, their dancers, and the audience to see just how profoundly different, or alike, the work could be. It was a symbolic white flag, a moment of respect, in the ongoing war between the modern and classical camps.

THE ENDURING MARTHA GRAHAM

Balanchine picked the music of Anton von Webern, a composer whose music was experimental and somewhat atonal. The composer used a broken melodic line and odd combinations of instruments, and made extremely brief compositions. A Webern symphony movement was often less than two minutes long. Balanchine's particular genius was for choreographing to the internal structure of music. He liked turning the mathematics of modern music into figures on stage. Graham also used modern music, but the composers she worked with most successfully, such as Aaron Copland in *Appalachian Spring*, gave her enough melodic line to use music as a way to shape characters and establish mood. She was not interested in making dances that looked like a geometry equation. She wanted emotion and high drama. Having risen to the challenge of performing back-to-back and face-to-face with New York City Ballet at City Center, Graham accepted Balanchine's music choice.

At 65 years of age, Graham was theoretically long past her dancing days. However, she could not give it up. Nothing in Graham's life mattered more to her than performing. Famously she had said, "The center of the stage is where I am."[50] Her highly dramatic approach to movement, with spectacular twisting falls to the ground and deep body contractions expressing yearning, were synonymous in most people's minds with modern dance. Balanchine's great contribution to classical ballet was to transform it into a sleek, abstract movement form we now call neoclassical ballet. He sometimes used stories and traditional sets and costumes, but only occasionally. The pure Balanchine style, with its high leg extensions, intricate footwork, and speed performed by dancers wearing black practice **leotards**, was as foreign to nineteenth-century classical ballet in its way as the Graham style.

Graham decided to base her dance on the historic standoff between Queen Elizabeth I of England and her cousin Mary, Queen of Scots. She staged it as a tennis match between the two, wherein Graham danced the role of Mary. She selected New York City Ballet dancer Sallie Wilson to perform the part of Queen Elizabeth, and two other male ballet dancers to hold up banners. Similarly, Balanchine asked that Paul Taylor—then dancing in the Graham company to great acclaim—perform a variation in his section. This was the extent of actual performance interaction between the modern camp and the ballet citadel.

The opening performance, on May 14, 1959, was a personal triumph for Graham. The audience spontaneously rose as soon as she appeared onstage. No one who saw Graham dance in her last years forgot the sheer force of personality on stage. She dominated stage space, obscuring both her age and limited physical abilities. Sixty-five years old or not, Graham's Mary was a commanding presence, and, at least in this danced version, Wilson's Elizabeth—a slight, much younger woman—was at a severe disadvantage. Although Graham's feet were crippled with arthritis and she could barely stand or walk, she danced magnificently. George Balanchine wisely stayed backstage and let Martha take the bows.

The critics weighed in with reviews that tended to favor whichever of the two geniuses they most admired. Those who disliked Balanchine saw his section as "inhuman" and "perverse." Graham's critics saw her section as "melodramatic" and "the same old steps."[51] *Episodes* was just that—an episode—and not the beginning of any true relationship between the two figures who as much as any were making the United States the world capital of dance.

Within a short time, *Episodes* would appear a quaint event. The 1960s were unfolding, and Balanchine was headed into his years of acknowledged greatness, when his work would come to dominate ballet. More important for modern dance, though, the Judson choreographers were beginning the experiments that would lead to yet another refocusing of modern dance. The emerging Post-Modernists would superficially appear the least likely candidates to bridge the gap between modern and ballet. What could be less balletic than dancing in sneakers or climbing a fire escape and calling it a dance?

THE VERSATILE TWYLA THARP

Yet, once again, modern dance was about to be jolted by someone trained from within. A Judson Dance Theater member from California named Twyla Tharp would introduce the first real artistic interchange between modern dance and ballet.

When Twyla Tharp arrived in New York City in 1961 as a mid-year transfer student at Barnard College, her major was art history, but her real interest was dance. As a child, she had studied ballet, tap, violin, and baton twirling with a self-imposed schedule of school, lessons, and practice that began at 6 A.M. with "Put practice clothes on" and ended more than 15 hours later at 9:30 P.M. with "Eat supper, get ready for bed."[52] As a young adult in New York City, Tharp's willpower remained as ferocious as ever. She combined lessons in ballet and every form of modern dance, offering classes with her college studies. She fell in love with Balanchine's work and would have studied at his School of American Ballet, but, as she wrote, "Fortunately his school was closed to the general public; had I been allowed access to

After arriving in New York City in 1961, Twyla Tharp immersed herself in dance. Tharp, who is pictured in 1975 rehearsing with an American Ballet Theatre dancer, has choreographed dances for many other dance troupes, including the Martha Graham Dance Company, the Royal Ballet, and the Joffrey Ballet.

Balanchine, I probably would have signed up for life and never developed my own idiom."[53]

Her classes ranged from ballet to Martha Graham and Merce Cunningham and even the Broadway jazz style of Bob Fosse. Tharp was accumulating an encyclopedic knowledge of different dance techniques and found the possibility of making out of "this swirling kaleidoscope of choices . . . a kind of a dance no one else could do."[54] Still an undergraduate at Barnard, Tharp focused on Paul Taylor and simply kept hanging around his studio until he put her in his company. Taylor described her as "a little person with enormous magnetism and push—a brash but lovable Munchkin."[55] She finished her Barnard degree but skipped graduation in order to go on tour with Taylor's company.

It was not long before Tharp began working on her own experimental dances, working in the Judson Church gym. Her first works were presented at Judson as well, but although her work looked like other products at Judson, philosophically it was different. Her 1966 *Re-Moves* was a four-section work performed in silence. It involved the dancers moving around a large plywood box, and then, in the final section, the dancers sat inside the box. After a long period of silence, they emerged, but not to take a bow. Tharp had declared that the audience was superfluous, and continued for five years instructing the dancers in her performances not to bow because, she explained, "I was worried, first, that there would be no audience, and second, that even if there was one, they would hate what we did."[56] Tharp herself saw *Re-Moves* as representing the bleakness of the Vietnam War era during which it was constructed. Even in works as challenging as this, Tharp was polishing an inclusive dance style that called for "trigger-quick shifts of weight from toe-to-heel, rapid changes of direction."[57] Her choreography compacted "innumerable slivers of movement." She resisted the Judson manifesto, saying that all the Judson no's—to spectacle, virtuosity, transformations, magic, and make-believe—"would become my yeses."[58]

In 1973, innovator Tharp happily accepted a commission from Robert Joffrey to create a new work for his Joffrey Ballet. This would be no *Episodes*, with ballet and modern greats performing cautiously and separately on the same stage space. This was Robert Joffrey, an innovative ballet director whose small troupe survived on an eclectic repertoire of twentieth-century ballets and newly commissioned dances, working with Twyla Tharp, a very flexible, imaginative choreographer who had made her name as a revolutionary who was well-grounded in ballet. Tharp would use some members of her own company (Twyla Tharp Dance), but they were making it happen for the Joffrey Ballet.

The result, *Deuce Coupe*, was set to the Beach Boys' pop songs that Tharp had grown up with in California. The backdrop was long paper rolls of original graffiti art. While the main body of the dance spilled across the stage with both Tharp and Joffrey dancers doing Tharp's quick changes between boogaloo, jazz, ballet, and modern steps, a solitary ballerina moved across the stage, methodically assuming many of the traditional positions of ballet. In a very interesting moment in dance and theater history, ballet visually intersected the modern dance realm. Tharp herself noted: "In 1959, Balanchine and Graham had shared a program . . . but my collaboration with the Joffrey marked the first time ever that a modern company performed in a ballet."[59] It was a critical and box-office hit.

Deuce Coupe was such a phenomenal success that Robert Joffrey quickly signed up Tharp to create another dance for his company, and eight months later in 1974, she presented *As Time Goes By*, danced to Haydn. Working with the Joffrey had its drawbacks though. The troupe survived by touring, and novelty is what brought audiences to see it. The Tharp pieces were huge novelties to audiences not used to ballet companies dancing to popular music or performing modern dance steps. Tharp thought she had made "well crafted dance(s), challenging and developing techniques and traditions . . ." but found the audiences were responding to bright lights, loud music, and "sexy people."[60]

The Joffrey successes were not ignored by the larger, more established ballet companies. The American Ballet Theatre (ABT) had recently hired Russian dancer Mikhail Baryshnikov, who had defected from the Soviet Union the summer of 1974. Baryshnikov was the latest in a series of spectacular ballet dancers who had fled from the Soviet's superb but highly institutionalized and confining ballet tradition. Rudolf Nureyev's defection to the West in 1961 had been the first, and he had electrified the ballet world and inspired a stream of other Soviet trained dancers to flee as well.

These dancers were magnificent talents, and they became cultural heroes in the Cold War-era standoff between the democracies of the

Mikhail Baryshnikov rehearses the Twyla Tharp ballet *Push Comes to Shove* at the Hollywood Bowl in Los Angeles in 1979.

West and the totalitarian Communist system of the East. They drew people to dance not simply to see their extraordinary abilities, but also to applaud their personal courage as well. When American Ballet Theatre approached Tharp about making a dance for Baryshnikov, she was initially hesitant. Here was a dancer being called one of the greatest, perhaps the greatest, to ever perform. Alvin Ailey said to her, "Are you going to do a ballet for Baryshnikov? You've got to be nuts. You'll be eaten alive."[61]

Baryshnikov, however, had not defected so that he could perform the same dances as those in the Russian repertory. He was in love with American culture, modern dance, and experimentation of all kind. The dancer he most admired was Fred Astaire. It was Baryshnikov himself who had suggested the Tharp commission after seeing what she had done for the Joffrey Ballet. He settled the question once and for all when Tharp came to watch him during an ABT rehearsal. He suddenly interrupted what he was doing to turn a cartwheel and do a somersault, landing literally at Tharp's feet. "Take me," he said. "I promise I'll never be boring or predictable."[62] One of the most intriguing partnerships in dance was born in that instant.

The dance Tharp made for Baryshnikov, *Push Comes to Shove*, was a mingling of everything imaginable—not just ballet and modern, but also jazz and ragtime and pure Tharp nonsense. She picked the name because it suggested the "juxtapositions in the ballet: the old classical forms of ballet versus jazz and its own classicism, the East of Misha [Baryshnikov's nickname], the West of Me . . . then too I knew it would please Misha: the name of the great Kirov instructor, responsible for Misha's development . . . was Aleksandr Pushkin."[63]

The dance premiered on January 9, 1976. Dancing to ragtime and Haydn, one of the greatest male dancers of all time was transformed into a "bowler-hatted, womanizing rogue." It was an astonishing success and established a partnership between Baryshnikov and Tharp that would be both personal and professional. Push really had come to shove in the dance world.

Essentially Twyla Tharp threw all the cards up in the air, catching and using those that suited her. She was not the first choreographer to shuffle steps from different dance techniques into one dance. Modern choreographers as early as Ruth St. Denis had been familiar with ballet technique and freely used ballet poses or turns in their work. Ballet dancers often danced in less formal classical works. Jerome Robbins's 1944 *Fancy Free*, a breezy, jazzy ballet of three sailors on leave in New York City, is only one of many examples.

What Tharp did differently was to blend steps together, stringing jazz, ballet, tap, and modern in one movement phrase. There was no signal she was changing from modern to ballet. A rolling modern Tharp torso shifted up into an airborne ballet *jeté* (leap in ballet in which one leg is extended forward and the other backward) and landed with the turned-in bent knees of jazz. She was not simply a modern choreographer who worked in ballet—she was a choreographer who threaded together steps from tap, ballet, modern, jazz, and ballroom seamlessly.

Push Comes to Shove was a defining moment in dance, and its effects are felt even now, more than 30 years later. By the late 1970s, the sharp divide between modern dance and ballet began to disappear. Yet, this did not mean that everyone was happy. Modern-dance purists scolded Tharp for abandoning her earlier experiments to work in "mainstream" ballet and theater. Ballet commentators worried that ballet was not producing enough of its own new choreographers and was relying too much on the modernists. Endless discussions have continued as to whether modern dancers or classical ballet dancers are better trained.

EXPERIMENTATION IN MODERN DANCE

This late 1970s experimentation was the beginning of what has come to be called the dance boom or dance explosion. Whether the audience started to come to dance performances to see a "novelty" dance or see a famous Russian or even out of simple curiosity turned out not to matter. An audience for dance was developing, one that was able to enjoy it as theater art, whether it understood the fine points of dance technique or a choreographer's philosophy. Audiences found that watching David Parsons appear to fly through the air as he danced in flickering strobe lights was thrilling enough, so that it did not matter whether they knew Parsons had danced with Paul Taylor's troupe and represented a line of modern dance tracing right back to Martha Graham.

The National Endowment for the Arts (NEA) established a dance touring program that sent smaller modern companies touring across the United States to perform in theaters and at universities. This was not vaudeville or a sequestered college summer session. Even when the dance touring program was cut back in the 1980s, companies continued to tour, having established audiences for their work across the country. American modern dance spread overseas, where important companies, including the Netherlands Dance Theater in The Hague and the

Frankfurt Ballet in Germany, have flourished with American dancers as artistic directors and choreographers.

Meanwhile, colleges and universities across the country included dance programs in their curriculum. Dance companies sprang up in the wake of the coursework and with the chance to see the professionals on tour. Students at Dartmouth College put together a funny, athletic, and professional troupe called Pilobolus, which specialized in contorting themselves into odd body sculptures onstage. Four more dance companies can claim descent from Pilobolus: Momix, Crowsnest, ISO, and BodyVox. If it is possible to see the Nikolais multimedia dance theater tradition in their work, it is not necessary or even intended.

In 1985—almost 25 years after David Gordon was making bizarre dances falling off chairs at Judson Church—Baryshnikov, then the American Ballet Theatre's artistic director, commissioned Gordon to do a work for the company. In Gordon's dance *Field, Chair, and Mountain*,

In 1971, students at Dartmouth College founded Pilobolus, an imaginative and athletic professional dance troupe. Named for a genus of fungi, Pilobolus is still prominent today. Here, Andrew Herro, Jeffrey Huang, and Manelich Minniefee perform as part of the troupe.

the ballet dancers carried around folding chairs that they opened and then arranged in ballet corps patterns. The dancers clambered up on the chairs and danced on them.

Totally abstract and experimental choreography continues as well. Judson dancer Steve Paxton experimented with a system of **contact improvisation**, where partners reacted to each other as the other moved. "Contact improv" started in dance studios and has entered into dance curriculum and is even performed as concert dance. It is almost like a game. Because the dancers slide and fall, needing to be caught or braced by the partner, it is more like an art sport. The tension for the dancers, and for anyone watching, resides in the trust the dancers must have in each other and how quickly they must respond. The partners constantly touch as "the inevitable result of leaning, sliding, twisting to follow the current of movement and play with the tug of gravity."[64]

Probably no dancer/choreographer gives a better picture of the state of modern dance in the early twenty-first century than Mark Morris. Morris was born in 1956, and his life mirrors the dance explosion. In the 1960s, while the Judson dancers were beginning their experiments, Morris was just a little boy in Seattle, Washington. This child loved to dance, and when he saw José Greco's Spanish dance troupe, he insisted on taking flamenco lessons. By the time he was 14 years old, Morris himself was teaching Spanish dance. In order to keep this hypertalented, hypercurious young man busy, his flamenco teacher directed him to ballet. He absorbed movement like a sponge. Then he became infatuated with Balkan folk dances and music, and, as a teenager, added a stint with the Koleda Folk Ensemble, a semiprofessional Balkan folk-dance company.

Because Morris was growing up in the era of the NEA dance touring program, living in Seattle did not prevent him from becoming familiar with companies such as Paul Taylor's, which visited regularly, or Martha Graham's. The Joffrey Ballet spent long weeks every summer in residence in the Seattle area, and Morris haunted their performances, especially loving the funky *Deuce Coupe* by Tharp.

By the time Morris began dancing professionally, he had trained and was interested in performing everything. That is exactly what he did. He performed in a ballet troupe (Eliot Feld), a modern dance company (Lar Lubovitch), and a Post-Modern ensemble (Laura Dean). He even worked with the outsized talent who started this whole wide-open dance scene, Twyla Tharp, when she choreographed the film *Hair* in 1979. In other words, Morris was the living exemplar of the almost un-limited possibilities of Post-Modern dance. When his own company (the Mark Morris Dance Group) had its first performance in 1980, it was held in Merce Cunningham's studio.

Gregarious, funny, and phenomenally talented, Morris fit in any-where. He was not a modern dancer who wanted to dance in silence or pick his music by chance. Since he openly relished everything from Romanian folk songs to Schubert, he quickly became noted as a choreog-rapher who also was a music connoisseur. As a performer, he physically managed to be a uniquely Post-Modern dancer as well. He is large—in fact, he is a huge, barrel-chested man, making him a very unlikely candi-date for a dancer. When Morris came onstage, it was like seeing a prepos-terous hippo in dance shoes. Then he would move and viewers saw that he was—in his own way—as elegant as Baryshnikov. Morris is openly gay in a very flamboyant way, which is a part of his stage persona. He plays with spoofs on cross-dressing, even costuming some of his male dancers in fluffy ballerina tutus but always in the context of the dance.

In 1991, Morris choreographed *The Hard Nut*, which is his version of ballet's Christmas classic *The Nutcracker*. It was created and first pre-sented at the Théâtre Royal de la Monnaie in Brussels, Belgium, when Morris was its dance artistic director. The generous resources of Bel-gium's national opera house were put at his disposal to create a sumptu-ous anti-*Nutcracker*. Morris set the Christmas party not in a lovely nine-teenth-century European mansion but in an ordinary 1960s American living room with white vinyl couches and a white plastic Christmas tree. The partygoers wear bell-bottomed pants and hot-colored minidresses. When the mysterious family friend Drosselmeier arrives, he does not present the heroine with toy soldiers and a dancing doll to entertain her. Instead, he brings robots and a life-sized Barbie. The traditional mock battle between the mice and the toy soldiers becomes a contest between big, hairy rats that fight G.I. Joes. In the "Waltz of the Snowflakes," both men and women—wearing fluffy white tutus and hats that look like the swirled tops of Dairy Queen ice cream cones—dance, and they all toss snowflakes merrily in the air. Morris himself danced the Arabian varia-tion at the opening, wearing slinky veils, ankle bells, and sunglasses.

One of the most prominent choreographers on the modern-dance scene today is Mark Morris. Known for his flamboyance and humor, Morris's first big hit was *The Hard Nut*, which debuted in 1991. Here, the Snowflakes dance during a performance of *The Hard Nut* at Zellerbach Hall, in Berkeley, California, in 2007.

The Hard Nut is outrageous, funny, and extravagantly inventive. It now plays annually in New York as an alternative to the better known traditional versions. This is how modern dance works—it is always personal art. It is a history of individual artists, each an intriguing personality. Some have the high drama of Martha Graham. Others seek the high plateau of Merce Cunningham's cerebral experimentation. Still others want to soar across stage like Paul Taylor, or see how it would work to add in hip-hop or Balinese moves.

There will be more of these original choreographers in the twenty-first century—stubborn yet talented people who will insist on working in their own unique ways. There undoubtedly will be a manifesto issued now and then. In its exuberance, ingenuity, and innovation, modern dance reflects the American spirit. Like jazz, hip-hop, and bluegrass, much of it was born here. Modern dance's story is one of expanding inclusion and equality, and it shows no sign of going away.

BEYOND FUSION: POP CULTURE GOES MAINSTREAM

Fusion brought one more significant change to what we call main stage contemporary dance. While modern and ballet choreographers were adding in **vernacular** moves to their choreography, vernacular performers—ordinary people, using their natural or ethnic dance styles—began constructing dances they intended to be performed on stage as well as in the neighborhood or community center. No longer content to provide intriguing accents to someone else's main stage work, they started companies of their own and began staging full evening performances using their own idiosyncratic movement vocabulary. What started as the fusion of different dance forms into mainstream modern and ballet companies transformed seamlessly into a profusion of new dance companies, working in totally different ways than the main stage dance troupes.

No one personifies the way contemporary dance has expanded its boundaries more than Rennie Harris, who grew up in North Philadelphia learning street dance moves and listening to the boom boom beat of the music. These loose-jointed and athletic moves to propulsive sound, whether instrumental or vocal, came to be called hip-hop. In 1992, Harris founded his company, Puremovement, which performs full evening stage events across the United States and Europe with all movement and sound being hip-hop. He wasn't just interested in moving; he wanted to change things. He wanted respect for the hip-hop movement and musical forms that shaped his own talent. He staged his own version of *Romeo and Juliet*, calling it *Rome and Jewels,* which includes a little Shakespeare, a lot of rap, and Juliet remaining offstage. Harris explains:

> We did a modernization of the text utilizing the language of hip-hop—the rapper's poetry. If you notice, rappers speak in rhythm. They speak indirectly and behind things. They switch words around or change their inflection, which changes the meanings of the words. That's called signifying. They take English language that stems from slave culture. Slaves created a way of talking to each other so that white people wouldn't understand what they were

saying. It had the same grammatical structure as many traditional African languages. Professors and scholars have written about this. We've carried our language rhythms with us over time. But because America is a big melting pot, no one wants to accept the fact that people hold on to their original language or aspects of it.[65]

Audiences now are used to dreadlock hair styles, dancers spinning around stage on one hand, and seeing a dancer's legs go one way while his torso flips off in an opposite direction. Even ballet choreographers look to hip-hop for movement inspiration. Trey McIntyre and Matthew Neenan are just two ballet choreographers who seamlessly twine hip-hop moves with ballet. This is not unlike the nineteenth-century ballet era, when folk dances were included in ballet productions staged in European opera houses for a mostly upper-class audience. The happy peasants dancing in *Giselle* or *Swan Lake* were a similar innovation in their own era.

The Irish dance troupe Riverdance is an example of the happy villagers taking their tradition of Irish step dancing (rapidly moving feet, an erect upper body) and turning it into a full evening performance for their own cultural benefit. Since its beginnings in 1994, Riverdance has spawned a host of smaller traditional dance troupes, although none of them have achieved the worldwide success of the original. In 2009, Riverdance announced it was sending three troupes into the world to perform in every theater where they have performed in their 15-year history. It was announced that at the tour's completion the company disbanded permanently.

Doris Humphrey wrote in 1959, "The dance has been, until recently, entirely ingénue, a sweet obedient child brought up in the theater and the court, and told to be young, pretty, and amusing. Steps and whole dances were borrowed for this infant from the lower classes (who were really inventive), and had their vulgarities removed so that kings and courtiers might find them acceptable for both performing and viewing."[66]

In the 1940s and 1950s, important choreographers were turning to lower class, even criminal class movement, as inspiration in creating mainstage theater. Agnes de Mille used American folk dance, square dance, tap (which began as a street performance form), and hoedown in the musical

Having first performed in 1994, Riverdance has become one of the most popular dance shows in the world. Here, dancers perform in Berlin in September 2007.

Oklahoma and her ballet *Rodeo*. When Jerome Robbins choreographed the 1957 musical *West Side Story*, which, like Harris's *Rome and Jewels*, drew its inspiration from Shakespeare's *Romeo and Juliet*—the story involved two opposing gangs in New York City. Like Harris's work, Robbins was using the movement of dance to convey the menace and violence of big-city gangs.

There are no longer any obedient children in dance. Twenty-first-century choreographers and dance companies revere its founders while constantly seeking new and inventive ways to stretch its skills and confound the audience. La La Human Steps, a Montreal-based troupe, has toured a version of *Swan Lake* entitled *Amjad,* an Arabic word that means either a male or a female. Edward Lock's choreography has both men and women dancing *en pointe* as swans, and Tchaikovsky's famous score is transformed and "punked up" by one of the most inventive music composers of the day, David Lang. This is not strictly modern dance because the company dances *en pointe,* but it clearly isn't classical ballet either.

Are all dance innovators either modern-dance choreographers or ballet choreographers? At this point in time, the most innovative of them are a bit of both. This is where fusion has taken dance. The most contemporary work being done today in any of the so-called disciplines involves rethinking what can and cannot be done on stage by dancers. In this way, Rennie Harris follows in Agnes de Mille's footsteps, and no one would be more interested in Harris's work than the feisty, opinionated de Mille. Edward Lock follows the tradition of Twyla Tharp when he tweaks our notions of dance partnering, but he owes a good deal to Ted Shawn, as well as to an all-male dance troupe called Ballets Trocadero de Monte Carlo, which has spent years putting on full-length parody performances of classics such as *Swan Lake*, while dressed in tutus and performing *en pointe*.

For more than 100 years, choreographers have created work that is based on personal experience, utilizing emerging technologies and ethnic traditions. This won't stop—it will simply become more and more diverse. This is what makes contemporary dance so exhilarating.

Choosing a Modern Dance Class

Girl or boy, gifted or clumsy, learn then, if you can, to dance. You will stand up straighter and walk prouder the rest of your life. And you will be kinder and more polite in all physical matters, and less afraid.

—Agnes de Mille[67]

There is nothing neat and tidy about studying modern dance. Unlike ballet—where one enters a beginning class and is instructed in the basic positions of the body, arms, legs, and feet in order to develop the movement vocabulary that a student ballet dancer will build on indefinitely—there is no standard introduction to modern dance. No fixed modern-dance terminology exists either, and confusingly enough, all modern-dance techniques use ballet terms, tap terms, and even jazz-dance terms to describe movements that may or may not be identical to the actual ballet, tap, or jazz-dance moves. This does not mean that there is no actual discipline of modern dance. Rather, it means that every modern dancer gets to experience something of the great exhilaration of the pioneering modern dancers as each finds his or her own way to dance.

Hundreds of modern dance styles are taught across the United States. Some focus on the technique of one major modern-dance figure. Most serious modern dancers have taken classes at one time or another in the techniques of Martha Graham, Limón-Humphrey, Lester Horton, Merce Cunningham, and Mary Wigman. These particular techniques are studied in part not only because the people were great dancers, but because they made movement systems that could be taught. Some of these are almost as formal and codified as ballet. Then there are brilliant instructors who have been influenced by Paul Taylor or Twyla Tharp or some other currently working modern choreographer who offer slightly different and still emerging approaches to modern dance. Any of these and countless other techniques can offer fine introductions to modern dance.

MODERN-DANCE CLASSES

To make matters even more complicated, the beginning modern dancer usually can find the option of taking a general introductory course on modern movement, often called Creative Dance or Expressive Movement. The quality of these courses ranges widely, but they usually emphasize work that centers the body through breathing and teaches how to move freely and comfortably on bare feet. A general creative dance class is often not very different from the kinds of freestyle, self-exploratory movement that Isadora Duncan and the early-twentieth-century adherents of eurythmics advocated.

In one way, a modern-dance class will be exactly like a ballet, tap, or jazz class. It will have a certain etiquette that is required of all students. The student will wear appropriate clothing for the class, and this includes footwear, if any. In most cases, the costume will be a leotard that enables the student to move freely and the instructor to easily see whether the student's movements are correct. Being prompt to every class is important. Every class will begin with some warm-up movements and then proceed to the increasingly more difficult and strenuous exercises. It is not possible to come in late and catch up, which is also rude to the instructor and the other students.

The dance teacher instructs by demonstrating and explaining the movement, and then the class will repeat this movement. Look for a

There are hundreds of modern dance styles taught throughout the United States, many of which blend ballet, tap dance, and even jazz dance. Here, members of a modern-dance class at the University of California at Los Angeles prepare for an upcoming performance.

class where the instructor is actively engaged in the students' work and is walking around, doing corrections both by talking and by actually physically moving a student's foot or shoulder into the correct place. There really is only one way to learn dance, and that is from another dancer, so corrections are essential. In most cases, the class takes place in a studio with a wall of mirrors. This allows the student as well as the instructor to focus on details of the movement. Good dancers are able to assess their own movements and make adjustments and corrections as they watch themselves. The studio will have a long *barre* along the wall for balance while students perform exercises on one side of the body. The *barre* is used primarily for ballet exercises and rarely with modern steps.

Class will be held to taped music, but it is not unusual for a modern-dance class to be accompanied by someone on piano and often with drums. Live accompaniment allows the instructor to stop and start the exercise as well as to change the tempo as the class moves along.

Modern-dance classes have been held to the sound of people reading poetry. When the class is finished, it is appropriate to give the instructor a round of applause before leaving the floor. This dance tradition comes from ballet, where class traditionally ends with a reverence, or bow, on the part of the students, followed by the students applauding the instructor. The structure of the dance lesson is a reminder to the student that the work is serious, and that those who wish to run, play, laugh, interrupt, and do whatever they want may do so only on their own time. A professional dancer is one of the most disciplined people in the world.

To select a modern-dance class, one must visit modern-dance classes offered in his or her local area. Classes are available in private studio classes, and in professional high schools for those in large metropolitan areas. There are many university and college dance departments, and these may offer opportunities, including public performances and seminars. If the student is near a city where touring companies perform, there will be chances to take master classes with the professionals just as Mark Morris did. In fact, if Morris's company is on tour, it would be possible to take classes with his company.

Sitting in on classes gives a prospective student an opportunity to get a feel for different techniques and to gauge his or her own reactions. Starting in one technique does not mean it is impossible to learn others in the future. Not every beginner feels ready to tackle a Martha Graham contraction. Since virtually every modern-dance instructor is different and usually a disciple of one particular technique, it is a good idea to visit before enrolling. The major techniques a prospective student is likely to find available include the following.

Martha Graham Classes

Martha Graham classes have four parts and are done on the center of the floor. They begin with floor work, which involves actually lying, as well as sitting, on the ground to do exercises intended to stretch and strengthen the torso. These include breathing exercises of inhaling and exhaling coordinated with contractions of the pelvic muscles, which are Graham's central movement device. There is nothing pedestrian about Graham movements; even the floor exercises are dramatic. The class proceeds to exercises standing in one place, which include **pliés** (knee bends) and **battement** (beats of the feet and legs). The ballet terminology is used, but the Graham dancer does not seek ballet's extreme **turnout** of the hip and feet. The class moves on to work with elevation (leaping), and finally with falling to the ground. Graham technique is full of falls, and she herself was famous for a spiral fall to the ground as treacherous to perform as it looked. Paul Taylor, Merce Cunningham, and Alwin Nikolais are only a handful of the important students of Graham technique.

Merce Cunningham Classes

Merce Cunningham classes begin in the center of the floor as well, but standing. Here the class does back stretches and *pliés*. There will be work on back curves, tilts, and twists. Attention will be given to exercises that increase feet articulation (the ability to use any part of your foot) and speed of footwork. Normally a Cunningham class does not do floor work, and it often looks like a ballet class, though the students are standing in the studio instead of working at an attached ballet *barre*. The movements have no inherent drama like Graham's but may be sped up or slowed down over and over to train the dancer to have the quickest possible response to movement. Cunningham's studio launched the Post-Modern Judson movement. His technique shares honors with Graham for being among the most influential in modern dance and is as abstract as Graham's is dramatic.

Lester Horton Classes

Lester Horton movement is very well known, even if his name may sound less familiar than Graham's or Cunningham's. Through his famous students (Alvin Ailey especially), the flat back projected forward into space with arms extending laterally is a movement image everyone recognizes. Like Graham's and Cuttingham's, Horton classes usually stay in the center of the floor, and only occasionally on the floor, with attention given to strengthening the torso. It is a very exhilarating as well as demanding way to move, and even the classes can look like a performance.

Limón-Humphrey Classes

Limón-Humphrey is the distillation of Doris Humphrey's fall-and-recovery movement theories. There are many important students of Limón-Humphrey (and Weidman) who, like the Horton students, have kept this more lyric modern-dance methodology alive. Doris Humphrey's philosophy remains at the core of the technique, stressing that emotion comes before movement. In addition to Humphrey's most famous student, José Limón, Sybil Shearer and Anna Halprin have passed on this way of moving to succeeding generations.

A serious modern-dance student usually studies ballet and tap. Sometimes it is helpful to do this before beginning modern-dance classes. All of the great modern dancers know the basic ballet steps and positions. The reason for this is simple: Ballet supplies a useful terminology

Choreographer Sara Rudner learned under Twyla Tharp and became the principal dancer for Tharp's dance company in 1966. Tharp's varied instruction played a major role in influencing Rudner's dance style. Here, dancers from Rudner's troupe perform *Dancing-on-View*, a six-hour improvisational dance, in New York City in 2007.

for all dancers. Even if modern dancers never attempt to have a fully turned-out leg, they will take classes and study choreography where they are asked to do something in a turned-out position. For a modern dancer, this means a comfortable turnout and not the extreme ballet position, which is only achieved even by ballet dancers after years of rigorous practice.

All modern-dance instructors scatter ballet terminology in their classes. Routinely, they ask a class to put their feet in second position, or even do a **tendu**. Just as routinely, they mix ballet with simple commands to move up or go down. Sometimes the instructor will ask for a *battement* and just as casually ask the dancers to lift their legs to the side, which is the same thing as a *battement*. In other words, ballet is dance's universal language, and it helps in any dance form one might study.

Tap is very useful for a modern dancer as well. Learning to create beats with the feet teaches the dancer about rhythm using his or her own body. Since the dancers are creating the beat and the sound, they experience sound and rhythm as a total body experience. This is different from dancing to music or even to drumming. If a modern dancer has any interest at all in going into jazz dance, he or she will find that the tap terms are jazz's basic vocabulary. A "ball and chain" is a tap sound that moves from the ball of one foot to the ball of another. It can be Twyla Tharp instructing: right ball change, *sur le* **cou-de-pied** on the left. Translated from tap and ballet, that means: shift your weight from the ball of the left foot to the right, and then place your right foot on the ankle of your left leg.

There are two magazines about dance that will help any modern-dance student. *Dance Magazine* is aimed at dance professionals and the general dance audience, and *Dance Spirit* is aimed at the student and young dance professional, as well as anyone interested in a dancer's world. Both magazines regularly list schools, summer sessions, camps, and other training opportunities. They have college issues and special sections on performing arts high schools, as well as listings for the professional giving auditions and job listings. If there are no modern-dance classes where the would-be student lives, the student can search these periodicals and write to information offices of modern-dance camps or short-term programs nearby to inquire about eligibility. Much of this, including checking the magazines, can be done online.

Modern dance is still about finding a personal way of moving, whether in the classroom or on the stage. There are people right now experimenting with new ideas for a dance. Maybe they are doing it in front of the mirror in their bedroom or twirling around and watching their reflection in the glass of a sliding door. These are people who think about movement. Sometimes they jump off a bus and add an extra hop just for the pleasure of doing it. They are movers. Fifty years from now, or even sooner, some of these preoccupied, dedicated, hardworking future dancer/choreographers will be added to yet another chapter of the history of modern dance.

CHRONOLOGY

1900   American experimental dancer Loie Fuller dances in her own pavilion at the Paris Exposition; American experimenters Isadora Duncan and Ruth St. Denis are in the audience.

1914   Ruth St. Denis selects Ted Shawn as dance partner; the two dancers subsequently marry in August of that year.

1915   Denishawn, the first important school teaching new dance methods, opens in Los Angeles, with the name created out of the names of founders Ruth St. Denis and Ted Shawn. The name Denishawn is used for their dance troupe as well.

1921   Isadora Duncan establishes dance institute in Soviet Union after period of fame in France.

1925–1926   Denishawn tours Japan, China, Burma, India, Ceylon (Sri Lanka), Malaya (Malaysia), Java, and the Philippines.

1926   Martha Graham, a former Denishawn dancer, performs her first independent solo dance concert.

1927   Isadora Duncan dies.

1928   Doris Humphrey and Charles Weidman, former Denishawn dancers, form their own troupe composed of other former Denishawn dancers and hold the first dance concert by a modern dance ensemble.

1929 Martha Graham premieres *The Heretic*, her first concert dance for a group of dancers.

1932 Lester Horton establishes a dance company in Los Angeles, which becomes the first fully racially integrated dance company in the United States.

1934 The Bennington College School of Dance summer program, the first important college program in modern dance, begins with instructors Martha Graham, Ruth Humphrey, Charles Weidman, and many other modern-dance pioneers on the faculty.

1944 Merce Cunningham, a member of the Martha Graham troupe, performs his first solo dance concert, with John Cage providing musical accompaniment.

1948 Lester Horton establishes the first theater in the United States dedicated solely to presenting dance.

1953 Merce Cunningham establishes his own dance company, with John Cage as musical director.

1954 Paul Taylor establishes his own modern dance troupe, the Paul Taylor Dance Company.

1957 Paul Taylor, a member of the Martha Graham troupe, presents *Seven New Dances*, which includes not moving to "non-music."

1958 Alvin Ailey, a Lester Horton dancer, establishes the Alvin Ailey American Dance Theater, continuing Horton's emphasis on inclusion, particularly in creating opportunities for African-American dancers and choreographers.

1960s   Beginning of Judson Dance Theater, a free-flowing and changing group of avant-garde dance experimenters working at a Greenwich Village church. They reject traditional technique and explore ordinary movement as dance.

1965   Twyla Tharp, at one time a Judson Theater experimenter, leaves the Paul Taylor Dance Company to form her own modern-dance company.

1976   Twyla Tharp choreographs *Push Comes to Shove* for Mikhail Baryshnikov at American Ballet Theatre in a successful blend of modern, ragtime-era popular dance, and ballet; it signals the beginning of a trend to assimilate a wide range of dance styles in one work.

1980s–present   This period is the Post-Modern dance explosion, although it is tapering off in recent years. Creative fusion of dance techniques leads to wide acceptance of experimental dance.

1992   Rennie Harris establishes Puremovement, a professional dance troupe devoted completely to hip-hop movement, performed to hip-hop music.

2002   Twyla Tharp choreographs *Movin' Out* for Broadway; in 2003, she wins two Tony Awards—for best choreography and direction.

2009   To celebrate the occasion of his 90th birthday, on April 16, Merce Cunningham premieres a full evening composition entitled *Almost Ninety*. Shortly after this final composition, Cunningham dies in July.

After a successful decade-and-a-half run, it is announced that the company of Riverdance will perform its final shows in 2010.

NOTES

CHAPTER 1

1 Isadora Duncan, *My Life.* (New York: Boni & Liveright, 1927; New York: Liveright, 1955), 3.

2 Peter Selz and Mildred Constantine, eds., *Art Nouveau, Art and Design at the Turn of the Century* (New York: Museum of Modern Art, 1975), 62.

3 Loie Fuller, *Fifteen Years of a Dancer's Life* (Boston: Small, Maynard & Co., 1913), 127.

4 Duncan, op. cit., 95.

5 Lincoln Kirstein, *Dance: A Short History of Classical Theatrical Dancing* (New York: G.P. Putnam's Sons, 1935; New York: Dance Horizons, 1977), 268.

6 Duncan, op. cit., 21.

7 Ibid., 3.

8 Agnes de Mille, *America Dances* (New York: Macmillan, 1980), 46.

9 Walter Sorell, *The Dance has Many Faces* (Cleveland and New York: World Publishing, 1951), 14.

CHAPTER 2

10 Ibid., 15.

11 Agnes de Mille, *Martha: The Life and Work of Martha Graham* (New York: Vintage Books, 1992), 41.

12 Jane Sherman, *Denishawn: the Enduring Influence* (Boston: Twayne Publishers, 1983), 17.

13 Ibid., 11.

14 de Mille, op. cit., 52.

15 de Mille, op. cit., 54.

16 Ruth St. Denis, *An Unfinished Life* (New York and London: Harper & Bros., 1939), 189.

17 Ibid., 191.

18 Sherman, op. cit., 63.

19 de Mille, op. cit., 68.

20 Martha Graham, *Blood Memory: An Autobiography* (New York and London: Doubleday, 1991), 91.

CHAPTER 3

21 Graham, op. cit., 6.
22 Ibid., 103.
23 Walter Terry, *Frontiers of Dance: The Life of Martha Graham* (New York: Thomas Crowell, 1975), 40.
24 Graham, op. cit., 68.
25 Ibid., 106.
26 Terry, op. cit., 49.
27 Graham, op., cit., 110.
28 Terry, op. cit., 59–60.
29 Graham, op. cit., 114.
30 Ibid.
31 Ibid.
32 Ibid.
33 Graham, op. cit., 117.
34 Olga Maynard, *American Modern Dance, The Pioneers* (Boston: Little Brown & Co., 1969), 127.
35 Ibid., 130.
36 Ibid., 131.
37 de Mille, op. cit., 102.
38 Maynard, op. cit., 143.
39 Elinor Rogisin, *The Dance Makers. Conversations with American Choreographers* (New York: Walker & Co., 1980), 16.
40 Sherman, op. cit., 41.
41 Terry, op. cit., 73.
42 José Limón, *An Unfinished Memoir* (Middletown, CT: Wesleyan University Press, 1998), 32.
43 Terry, op. cit., 62.

CHAPTER 4

44 Richard Kostelantz, ed., *Merce Cunningham: Dancing in Space and Time* (Pennington, NJ: A Cappella Books, 1992), 39.
45 Edwin Denby, "Elegance in Isolation." *Looking at the Dance* (New York: Popular Library, 1968), 303–304.
46 Joan Acocella, "Twos and Threes." *The New Yorker.* (May 4, 2009), 77.
47 Deborah Jowitt, *The Dance in Mind* (Boston: David Godine, 1985), 199.
48 Paul Taylor, *Private Domain* (San Francisco: North Point Press, 1988), 80.

CHAPTER 5

49 Twyla Tharp, *Push Comes to Shove* (New York: Bantam Books), 3.

50 Graham, op. cit., 69.

51 Taylor, op. cit., 94.

52 Ibid., 30.

53 Ibid., 47–48.

54 Ibid., 54.

55 Taylor, op. cit., 161.

56 Tharp, op. cit., 89.

57 Don McDonagh, *The Rise and Fall of Modern Dance* (New York: Mentor Book, 1970), 109.

58 Tharp, op. cit., 88–89.

59 Ibid., 177–178.

60 Ibid., 185–186.

61 Ibid., 205.

62 Ibid.

63 Ibid., 218.

64 Jowitt, op. cit., 336.

65 Rose Eichenbaum, *Masters of Movement: Portraits of America's Great Choreographers,* (Washington, D.C.: Smithsonian Books, 2004), 158.

66 Doris Humphrey, *The Art of Making Dances* (New York: Rinehart, 1959; Princeton, NJ: Princeton Book Co., 1987), 15.

CHAPTER 6

66 Agnes de Mille, *To A Young Dancer: A Handbook* (Boston: Little Brown & Co. 1962), 12.

GLOSSARY

ballet   From the Italian *ballare*. As theatrical dance, it is an art form based on a specific technique involving a fixed set of steps and positions developed over hundreds of years. Nonspecifically, the term is used by all choreographers to describe a concert dance. For example, it would not be incorrect to call Alvin Ailey's dance *Revelations* a ballet, although it actually is modern dance.

barre   A horizontal wooden handrail used by dancers to maintain balance while doing studio exercises. It is used by both modern and ballet dancers, but principally in classical ballet classes. A ballet dancer places one hand lightly on the *barre* while doing exercises that require balance.

battement   A beating movement of an extended leg or foot. This is a ballet term but is widely used in all forms of dance.

choreography   From Greek, literally meaning "dance-writing." It is the steps and patterns of a particular dance. The person who designs the steps and patterns is called the choreographer.

contact improvisation   A playful improvisation between two or more dancers in which they respond to each other's movement as it occurs in the moment. Thus, dancers must react very quickly to protect themselves from falling or slipping if not instantaneously supported. Often called "art sport." Steve Paxton, a Judson Theater experimenter, is credited with creating the movement form.

contraction-release   The fundamental movement of the Martha Graham technique. It refers to movement in the torso as the dancer inhales (contracts) and exhales completely (releases).

cou-de-pied   A ballet position that puts the working foot on the ankle of the supporting leg. The term is used in other dance forms as well.

Dalcroze   Émile Jaques-Dalcroze (1865–1950) was a student of Francois Delsarte. He furthered the Desarte method by designing a system of training music students to understand rhythm by translating sounds into physical movements. It could be, and was, applied to dance as well and influenced many early modern dancers. He called the system "rhythmic gymnastics," and it became known as eurythmics.

Delsarte   François Delsarte (1811–1871) was a French music teacher in the early nineteenth century who developed a system known as the Delsarte method, in which performers were taught to develop the expressiveness of their bodies. He placed his movements into three categories (eccentric, concentric, and normal) and three zones (head, torso, and limbs). It was a very influential methodology for all the early modern-dance pioneers, as well as for several generations of gymnasts and students of calisthenics.

eurythmics   Rhythmic gymnastics created by Emile Jaques-Dalcroze, sometimes called the Dalcroze system. *See Dalcroze.*

German Expressionism   In the early twentieth century, Expressionism dominated the arts in Germany and Central Europe. The artist stressed the emotional content of experience and symbolic meaning in objects. In dance, these ideas were explored by Mary Wigman (1886–1973), among others, who taught and performed a technique emphasizing dramatic intensity and distortion of body shapes. Wigman was one of the most important pioneers of modern dance, but her career was interrupted when she was condemned by the Nazis and forced to shut down her schools. She did not resume teaching and performing until 1949.

hip-hop   A music genre that uses a rhythmic vocal style called rap, which is accompanied by heavy beats. Hip-hop originated in African American communities on the East and West Coasts. Each version is slightly different from the other, but both emphasize rhyming, strong beats, and fearless physical movement often performed on sidewalks. Hip-hop, which began in the 1970s, has now been around long enough to have more than one style.

leotard   A tight garment covering the torso, usually worn over tights. It is the basic practice costume for any dance study. There actually was a man named Jules Léotard, a French gymnast who is credited with creating the costume.

modern dance   An unsatisfactory term usually used to describe any experimental concert dance that is not classical ballet or ethnic/folk dance. It was considered an old-fashioned term by the 1940s, when even Martha Graham called her company Martha Graham Contemporary Dance. The term still continues, largely out of common usage.

plié   A bend of the knee, often in preparation for jumps or turns. This is a ballet term, widely used in all forms of dance.

Post-Modern   A catch-all phrase covering experimental dance from Merce Cunningham to the present. Essentially, it separates the post-Cunningham experimenters from the so-called historic modern dancers. Generally, it favors abstraction of content, the cerebral over the highly emotional, and movement representing many techniques. It can, however, include any and all of the above as well.

tendu   Short for *battement tendu*, a ballet term for any move by the working foot, with the working toes on the floor and the legs straight and stretched; used widely in other dance forms.

turnout   The outward rotation of the legs from the hips at a 90-degree angle. Turnout enables a dancer to move quickly to either side of the body as well as forward and backward without breaking the line of the leg. A ballet position widely used in all forms of dance.

tutu   A ballerina's traditional costume consisting of a projecting skirt made of many layers of net or tulle. It is derived from a French slang term meaning "backside."

vernacular   A term meaning "native" or "of the people." It can refer to everything from architecture (houses made with local materials in functional styles suited to ordinary people) to spoken language and word choices (English as opposed to Latin, which is no longer a vernacular language but one of liturgy and literature).

BIBLIOGRAPHY

Acocella, Joan. *Twenty-Eight Artists and Two Saints: Essays.* New York: Vintage Books, 2007.

Anderson, Jack. *Choreography Observed.* Iowa City: University of Iowa Press, 1987.

Au, Susan. *Ballet and Modern Dance.* London: Thames and Hudson, 1988.

Banes, Sally. *Terpsichore in Sneakers, Post Modern Dance.* Boston: Houghton Mifflin, 1980.

Bird, Dorothy, and Joyce Greenberg. *Bird's Eye View: Dancing with Martha Graham and on Broadway.* Pittsburgh: University of Pittsburgh Press, 1997.

Chujoy, Anatole. *The Dance Encyclopedia.* New York: Barnes & Co., 1949.

Cohen, Selma Jeanne, ed. *Dance as a Theater Art: Source Readings in Dance History from 1581 to the Present.* New York: Harper & Row, 1974.

Constantine, Mildred, and Peter Selz, eds. "Art Nouveau: Art and Design at the Turn of the Century." *Art Journal,* vol. 20, no. 4 (Summer, 1961), pp. 256–258 New York: Museum of Modern Art.

Crain, Debra, and Judith MacKrell. *Oxford Dictionary of Dance.* Oxford, UK: Oxford University Press, 2000.

Current, Richard Nelson, and Marcia Ewing Nelson. *Loie Fuller: Goddess of Light.* Boston: Northeastern University Press, 1997.

de Mille, Agnes. *America Dances.* New York: MacMillan, 1980.

———. *Martha: The Life and Work of Martha Graham.* New York: Vintage Books, 1992.

———. *To a Young Dancer: A Handbook.* Boston: Little Brown & Co., 1962.

Denby, Edwin. *Dancers, Buildings, and People in the Street.* New York: Popular Library, 1979.

———. *Looking at the Dance.* New York: Popular Library, 1968.

Duncan, Isadora. *My Life.* New York: Boni & Liveright, 1927. Reprint, New York: Liveright, 1955.

Eichenbaum, Rose. *Masters of Movement: Portraits of America's Great Choreographers.* Washington, DC: Smithsonian Books, 2004.

Foulkes, Julia. *Modern Bodies: Dance and American Modernism from Martha Graham to Alvin Ailey.* Chapel Hill and London: University of North Carolina Press, 2002.

Fuller, Loie. *Fifteen Years of a Dancer's Life.* Boston: Small, Maynard & Co., 1913.

Graham, Martha. *Blood Memory: An Autobiography.* New York and London: Doubleday, 1991.

Humphrey, Doris. *The Art of Making Dances.* New York: Rinehart, 1959. Reprint, Princeton, NJ: Princeton Book Co., 1987.

Jacob, Ellen. *Dancing: A Guide for the Dancer.* Reading, Mass. and Menlo Park, CA: Addison-Wesley Publishing Co., 1981.

Jowitt, Deborah. *The Dance in Mind.* Boston: David Godine, 1985.

———. *Time and the Dancing Image.* New York: William Morrow, 1988.

Kirstein, Lincoln. *Dance: A Short History of Classical Theatrical Dancing.* New York: G.P. Putnam's Sons, 1935. Reprint, New York: Dance Horizons, 1977.

Kostelanetz, Richard, ed. *Merce Cunningham: Dancing in Space and Time.* Pennington, N.J.: A Cappella Books, 1992.

Kozodoy, Ruth. *Isadora Duncan.* New York: Chelsea House Publishers, 1988.

Kraus, Richard. *History of the Dance.* Englewood Cliffs, NJ: Prentice Hall, 1969.

Limón, José. *Unfinished Memoir.* Middletown, Conn.: Wesleyan University Press, 1998.

McDonagh, Don. *Complete Guide to Modern Dance.* New York: Popular Library, 1977.

———. *The Rise and Fall and Rise of Modern Dance.* New York: Mentor Book, 1970.

Martin, John. *The Modern Dance.* 1933. Reprint, New York: Dance Horizons, 1965.

Maynard, Olga. *American Modern Dancers: The Pioneers.* Boston: Little Brown & Co., 1969.

Penrod, James, and Janice Gudde Plastino. *The Dancer Prepares: Modern Dance for Beginners,* 4th ed. Palo Alto, CA: Mayfield Publishers, 1992.

Reynolds, Nancy, and Susan Reimer-Torn. *Dance Classics: A Viewer's Guide to the Best-Loved Ballets and Modern Dances.* New York: Harmony Books, 1980. Reprint, Chicago: A Cappella Books, 1991.

Robertson, Allen, and Donald Hutera. *The Dance Handbook*. Boston: G. K. Hall, 1988.

Rogosin, Elinor. *The Dance Makers: Conversations with American Choreographers*. New York: Walker & Co., 1980.

Roseman, Janet Lynn. *Dance Masters: Interviews with Legends of Dance*. New York: Routledge, 2001.

St. Denis, Ruth. *An Unfinished Life*. New York & London: Harper and Bros, 1939.

Seroff, Victor. *The Real Isadora*. New York: The Dial Press, 1971.

Shelton, Suzanne. *Divine Dancer: A Biography of Ruth St. Denis*. New York: Doubleday, 1981.

Sherman, Jane. *Denishawn: The Enduring Influence*. Boston: Twayne Publishers, 1983.

Sorell, Walter. *The Dance Has Many Faces*. Cleveland and New York: World Publishing Co., 1951.

Taylor, Paul. *Private Domain*. San Francisco: North Point Press, 1988.

Terry, Walter. *Frontiers of Dance: The Life of Martha Graham*. New York: Thomas Y. Crowell, 1975.

Tharp, Twyla. *Push Comes to Shove*. New York: Bantam Books, 1992.

FURTHER RESOURCES

BOOKS

Au, Susan. *Ballet and Modern Dance*. London: Thames and Hudson, 1988.

de Mille, Agnes. *Martha: The Life and Times of Martha Graham*. New York: Vintage Books, 1992.

Duncan, Isadora. *My Life*. New York: Liveright, 1955.

Graham, Martha. *Blood Memory: An Autobiography*. New York and London: Doubleday, 1991.

Kozodoy, Ruth. *Isadora Duncan*. New York: Chelsea House Publishers, 1988.

Limón, José. *An Unfinished Memoir*. Middletown, CT: Wesleyan University Press, 1998.

Shelton, Suzanne. *Divine Dancer: A Biography of Ruth St. Denis*. New York: Doubleday, 1981.

Taylor, Paul. *Private Domain*. San Francisco: North Point Press, 1988.

Tharp, Twyla. *Push Comes to Shove*. New York: Bantam Books, 1992.

VIDEOGRAPHY

Modern Dance: The Founders and the Historic Generation

Charles Weidman: On His Own, 60 minutes, Dance Horizons Video, 1990. Narrated by Alwin Nikolais. A lovingly crafted documentary that takes Weidman from Nebraska to Denishawn, and then on through his partnership with Doris Humphrey and his own work. Includes footage of Weidman performing with Humphrey, as well as Weidman talking about his work and teaching.

The Dance Works of Doris Humphrey, a two-part video documenting work of this important dance pioneer.

Part I: *With My Red Fires* and *New Dance*, 60 minutes, Dance Horizons Video, 1989. Performed by the American Dance Festival Company, these two dances from the mid-1930s deal, respectively, with conflict between the sexes, and conflict between the individual and the group.

Part II: *Ritmo Jondo* and *Day On Earth*, 40 minutes, Dance Horizons Video, 1999. These works are danced by the José Limón Dance Company, which performs Humphrey's choreography to this day, not as historic relics but as living dance.

Denishawn: Birth of Modern Dance, 40 minutes, Kultur Video, 1988. Contains historic film as well as recent reconstructions. Performed by Center City Collective, a dance troupe dedicated to the preservation of Denishawn material.

Denishawn Dances On!, 100 minutes, Kultur Video, 2002. With twenty-three dances performed by Denishawn Repertory Dancers, this is the largest re-creation of Denishawn material in existence. Pulled together by Barton Mumaw, member of Denishawn in its last year, and Jane Sherman, last living member of the original company.

Martha Graham Dance Company, 60 minutes, WNET/Dance in America Production, 1998. This 1976 television broadcast was choreographed by and produced under Martha Graham herself. Dancers include Janet Eilber, Yuriko Kimura, and others from one of Graham's finest group of dancers.

Martha Graham in Performance, 93 minutes, Kultur Video, 1988. Graham narrates and introduces her company performing three important works, including *Night Journey* with Graham as Jocasta and Paul Taylor as Tiresius.

Martha Graham: The Dancer Revealed, 90 minutes, Kultur Video, 1994. Considered the definitive video record of Graham's work, it includes historic footage of her most famous work, including *Heretic*, *Lamentations*, and *Appalachian Spring*, as well as clips of Graham talking about her work. Graham's former husband Erick Hawkins, biographer and fellow dance innovator Agnes de Mille, and several Graham dancers are interviewed.

Mary Wigman, 1886–1973: "When Fire Dances between Two Poles," 41 min., Dance Horizons Video, 1990. Famous German Expressionist dance innovator Wigman discusses her work (English voiceover). Film includes rare footage of Wigman's last performance, which was in 1942.

Modern Dance: Reformers

Cage/Cunningham, 95 minutes, Kultur Video, 1991. A collage of interviews and excerpts from the work of the important partnership of choreographer Merce Cunningham and composer John Cage. Dancer Rudolf Nureyev and artist Robert Rauschenberg are among fellow artists included.

A Lifetime of Dance with Merce Cunningham and His Dance Company, 90 minutes, Winstar Home Entertainment, 2000. New and archival performances. A coproduction of Thirteen/WNET New York and BBC.

Paul Taylor Dance Company: Esplanade/Runes, 58 minutes, WNET/Dance in America, 1998. Performed by Paul Taylor and company and recorded in 1977. Part of the PBS "Dance in America" series.

Paul Taylor: Dancemaker, 98 minute, Artistic License, 1998. Nominated for an Academy Award in 1999 for Short Subject. One of the best dance documentaries ever made and certainly an unusually good dance video; candid, biographical, and inspiring, *Dancemaker* follows Taylor's entire career.

Points in Space, 55 minutes, Kultur Video, 1986. Featuring Cunningham Dance Company. Interviews, behind-the-scenes footage, as well as performance.

The World of Alwin Nikolais, Pro Arts International, 1996. Directed and narrated by Murray Louis. Performed by Murray Louis and dancers, *The World of Alwin Nikolais* is a five-part series that re-creates Nikolais's original stage presentations. Each part is approximately 40 minutes long, and they can be purchased separately or as a set.

Modern Dance: Fusion

Baryshnikov Dances Sinatra and More, 60 minutes, Kultur Video, 1985, videocassette. Baryshnikov, Tharp, and American Ballet Theatre dancers perform, including the epoch-making *Push Comes to Shove*, as well as *The Little Ballet* and *Sinatra Suite*. Originally part of the PBS "Dance in America" series.

Four By Ailey, 140 minutes, Kultur Video, 1986. Performed by the Alvin Ailey American Dance Theatre. An important record of Ailey's masterpiece *Revelations,* as well as other major dances.

Pilobolus Dance Theatre, 59 minutes, WNET/Dance in America, 1998. Four dances by this influential small troupe that began at Dartmouth College, part of the PBS "Dance in America" series.

A Tribute to Alvin Ailey, 120 minutes, Kultur Video, 1989. Dance special featuring the Alvin Ailey Dance Theatre honoring its founder and introduced by dancer Judith Jamison, who succeeded Ailey as artistic director of the troupe after Ailey's death in 1989.

WEB SITES

Alvin Ailey American Dance Theater

www.alvinailey.org

This is the official Web site of the Alvin Ailey's dance troupe, which is the premier dance company for African American modern dance.

Dance

www.dancemagazine.com

The renowned dance magazine's Web site includes back issues, reviews, forums, videos, and blogs.

Dance Spirit

www.dancespirit.com

The Web site for *Dance Spirit* magazine includes a directory of dance schools and a chat room.

David Parsons

www.parsonsdance.org

This is the site for the dance trouped headed by David Parsons, who has choreographed more than 70 works for the group.

The Doris Humphrey Society

www.dorishumphrey.org

Information about famed modern dancer Doris Humphrey, including workshops and upcoming performances of her works, can be found here.

Isadora Duncan Dance Foundation

www.isadoraduncan.org

This site provides information on the Isadora Duncan dance company, foundation, and classes and workshops.

Jacob's Pillow

www.jacobspillow.org

Find information about the famous summer dance festival founded by Ted Shawn, school, archives, and community programs.

Jerome Robbins Dance Division, New York Public Library
for the Performing Arts

http://www.nypl.org/research/lpa/dan/dan.html

The New York Public Library's collection of modern-dance documents and photos is the largest and most comprehensive archive of its kind in the world.

José Limón Dance Foundation

www.limon.org

Information about renowned Mexican modern dancer/choreographer José Limón, including classes and videos, can be found here.

Mark Morris Dance Group

www.mmdg.org

This site offers information about the Brooklyn-based school, dance center, and company of one of the most successful choreographers of today.

Martha Graham Center of Contemporary Dance

www.marthagrahamdance.org

The site for the oldest and most celebrated modern dance company in the world provides information about Martha Graham, the company, and the school.

Merce Cunningham Dance

www.merce.org

The official Web site of renowned modern-dancer/choreographer Merce Cunningham includes video of dance classes taught by Cunningham.

Paul Taylor Dance Company

www.ptdc.org

The official Web site of the Paul Taylor Dance Company features biographical information on Taylor and the dancers, as well as information on daily classes and summer intensive programs.

Pilobolus

www.pilobolus.com

This is the official site for the modern-dance group, founded at Dartmouth College in 1971.

Rennie Harris Puremovement

www.rhpm.org

This Philadelphia dance troupe preserves and disseminates hip-hop culture through workshops, classes, lecture-demonstrations, dance residencies, mentoring programs, and public performances.

Riverdance

www.riverdance.com

The official Web site of the ultra-successful Irish step-dance group features photos, biographies, tour dates, and a message board.

Twyla Tharp Dance

www.twylatharp.org

The official Web site of the Tony Award–winning choreographer Twyla Tharp includes photos and biographical information about her.

PICTURE CREDITS

PAGE

15: © INTERFOTO/Alamy

20: Archives Charmet/The
Bridgeman Art Library

24: © Bettmann/Corbis

29: E. O. Hoppe/Mansell/Time
Life Pictures/Getty Images

34: © Pictorial Press Ltd/Alamy

41: © Corbis

46: © Bettmann/Corbis

49: © Interphoto/Alamy

52: © Time & Life Pictures/
Getty Images

55: © Time & Life Pictures/
Getty Images

56: © Time & Life Pictures/
Getty Images

61: © Bettmann/Corbis

66: © Hulton-Deutsch
Collection/Corbis

71: © Time & Life Pictures/
Getty Images

74: © Time & Life Pictures/
Getty Images

77: © AFP/Getty Images

80: © Katy Raddatz/San Francisco Chronicle/Corbis

83: © Getty Images

87: © Phil Schermeister/Corbis

90: © Getty Images

INDEX

A

Abstract Expressionism, 59
ABT. *See* American Ballet Theatre
African-American themes, 55
Ailey, Alvin, 19, 56–57, 66–67, 74, 89
Alcestis, 60
American Ballet Theatre (ABT), 73–75, 77–78
American Repertory Theater, 65
Amjad, 19, 83
Annie Get Your Gun, 55
Appalachian Spring, 51–52, 57
Art Nouveau, 16–17
arthritis, 45, 54
articulation, 89
Astaire, Fred, 75
So the Audience Does Not Know Whether I Have Stopped Dancing (Brown), 64–65
audiences, 72

B

back-lighting, 19
Balanchine, George, 8, 39, 68–70, 71

Balkan folk dances, 78
Ball, Mary Washington, 37
ballet, 14, 39, 53, 68–76, 90–91
Ballets Trocadero de Monte Carlo, 84
Barnard College, 71–72
barre, 87, 89
Baryshnikov, Mikhail, 73–76, 77–78
battement, 89, 91
Beach Boys, 73
Bennington College, 48–50, 54
Berkeley, University of California at, 32–33
Beyer, Hilda, 28
The Birth of a Nation, 34
black dance, 56
BodyVox, 77
Bolshevik revolution, 23
breathing, 42–43, 88
Brice, Fanny, 35
Brooks, Louise, 34
Brown, Trisha, 63, 64–65

C

Cabaret, 54
Cage, John, 57, 59, 61
Camelot, 56
car accidents, 22–23
Castle, Irene and Vernon, 25

Caught (Parsons), 18–19
chance, 57
Chicago, 54
Childs, Lucinda, 63, 65
Clair de Lune (Graham), 42
classes, overview of, 86–91
Clytemnestra, 60
Colorado College, 56
Communism, 23
contact improvisation, 78
contraction-release breathing, 42–43, 88
Coolidge Foundation, 51
Coolidge Theatre, 51
Copeland, Aaron, 51–52
Creative Dance classes, 86–88
Crowsnest, 77
Cunningham, Merce, 51, 57–59, 66, 67, 89

D

Dalcroze, Émile, 16, 22
Dance Magazine, 91
Dance Repertory Theater, 48, 54
Dance Spirit, 91
dance theater, 60
Danse Americaine, 47
Dartmouth College, 77
de Mille, Agnes, 34, 39, 45, 82

de Mille, Cecil B., 34
Dean, Laura, 63
debt, 33
Delsarte method, 30
Denishawn
    end of, 35–38
    fabric and, 19
    origins of, 28–31
    overview of, 25–26
    spread of, 31–32
    success of, 32–35
    Weidman and, 47
Denishawn School, 28–31
Dennis, Ruth. *See* St.
    Denis, Ruth
Deuce Coupe (Tharp),
    73, 78
Diaghilev, Serge, 39
Dolin, Anton, 37
Duet, 61
Duncan, Isadora, 14, 17,
    21–23, 32, 39
Dunham, Katherine, 56

E

Eastman, George, 42
Eastman School of Music,
    42
Egypta (St. Denis), 30
Elizabeth I (Queen of
    England), 69–70
emotions, 8–9, 21
emotive dance, 21–22
Epic (Taylor), 62
Episodes, 68–70
equilibrium, 44–45
Esplanade (Taylor), 62
eurythmics, 16, 22
The Event of the Year, 9–10
Expressive Movement
    classes, 86–88

F

fabric, illusion and, 18–19
facial expressions, 30
Fairbanks, Douglas, 34

Fancy Free (Robbins), 75
Federal Dance Project,
    55, 56
Field, Chair, and Mountain
    (Gordon), 77–78
Florentine Madonna
    (Graham), 42
Folies Bergère, 16
foot position, 43
Forti, Simone, 63
Forty-Eighth Street
    Theater, 42
Fosse, Bob, 54
Frankfurt Ballet, 77
Fuller, Loie, 13–18, 22

G

The Garden of Kama
    (Denishawn), 32
German Expressionism,
    50, 56, 60
Germany, 22
gestures, 30
Gordon, David, 63–64, 65,
    77–78
Graham, Martha
    after Denishawn, 40–44
    Appalachian Spring
        and, 51–52, 57
    Bennington College
        and, 50
    dance classes and,
        88–89
    Dance Repertory
        Theater and, 48
    death of, 45
    Denishawn and, 31, 35,
        36–38
    Episodes and, 68–70
    fabric and, 19
    Presidential Medal of
        Freedom and, 67
    retirement of, 54
    Taylor and, 60
Great Depression, 38, 40,
    50, 55

Greco, José, 78
Greek Theatre, 32–33
Greenwich Village Follies,
    40
Griffith, D.W., 34
Guthrie Theater, 65
gymnastics, 16

H

Hair, 79
Halprin, Anna, 90
The Hard Nut (Morris),
    79–80
Harris, Rennie, 37, 81–82,
    84
Hawkins, Erick, 51
Heretic (Graham), 43
Hill, Martha, 48
hip-hop, 37, 82
Hitler, Adolf, 40
Holm, Hanya, 50, 54–55,
    56
homosexuality, 36, 79
Horst, Louis, 31, 36–37,
    42, 62
Horton, Lester, 56–57,
    66, 89
How Long Brethren?
    (Tamiris), 55
La La La Human Steps,
    19, 83
humor, 44, 47
Humphrey, Doris
    Bennington College
        and, 50
    Dance Repertory
        Theater and, 48
    Denishawn and, 31,
        36, 38
    Limón-Humphrey
        classes and, 90–91
    overview of, 44–47
    retirement of, 54
Humphrey-Weidman
    Group, 44, 54

I

illusion, dance as, 18–19
improvisation, 78
internet, 59
Intolerance, 34
Isadora. *See* Duncan, Isadora
Isis, 25
ISO, 77

J

Jacob's Pillow, 36–37, 38, 48
Jacques-Dalcroze, Émile. *See* Dalcroze, Émile
jazz, 91
jeté, 75
Joel, Billy, 65
Joffrey, Robert, 72–73
Joffrey Ballet, 72–73
Johnston, Julianne, 34
Jones, John Paul, 58
José Limón Dance Company, 54
Judson Dance Theater, 63–66

K

Kennedy, John F., 62
King, Martin Luther Jr., 62
Kiss Me Kate, 56
Koleda Folk Ensemble, 78
Kosugi, Takehisa, 58

L

La La La Human Steps, 19, 83
La Loie. *See* Fuller, Loie
L'Ag'ya (Dunham), 56
Lamentation (Graham), 19, 44
Lang, David, 83
Legion d'Honneur, 67
Letter to the World, 57

Life of the Bee (Humphrey), 45
Limón, José, 44, 45, 48, 54
Limón-Humphrey classes, 90–91
lithographs, 17
Lock, Edward, 83, 84
La Loie. *See* Fuller, Loie

M

magazines, 91
Male Dancers, 36–37, 38, 48
Mamoulian, Rouben, 42
Man Walking Down the Side of a Building (Brown), 65
March Slav (Duncan), 23
Mark Morris Dance Group, 79
Markova, Alicia, 37
Martinique, 56
Mary, Queen of Scots, 69–70
Masks, Props, and Mobiles (Nikolais), 60
McIntyre, Trey, 82
Michael (student), 9–11
mime, 44, 47
Momix, 77
Monk, Meredith, 63
Morris, Mark, 78–80, 88
movement theory, 30
movie industry, 33–34
Movin' Out (Tharp), 65
music, 45–46
musical visualizations, 32
Mussolini, Benito, 40
My Fair Lady, 56
mysticism, 25

N

National Dance Institute, 9
National Endowment for the Arts (NEA), 76, 78

National Medals of Arts, 67
Native American culture, 56
NEA. *See* National Endowment for the Arts
Nearly Ninety, 57–59
Neenan, Matthew, 82
Negro Spirituals (Tamiris), 55
Netherlands Dance Theater, 76
New York Palace, 35
Nijinsky, Vaslav, 39
Nikolais, Alwin, 56, 59–60, 66
Non Score (Taylor), 61
Nureyev, Rudolf, 73
The Nutcracker, 79

O

Oklahoma, 82
One Thousand and One Night Stands (Shawn), 36
online dance companies, 59
opera, 65

P

pageants, 32–33
Panama California Exposition, 33
Pantages vaudeville circuit, 34
Paris Exposition of 1900, 13
parody, 84
Parsons, David, 18–19, 76
Pavlova, Anna, 39
Paxton, Steve, 78
Picasso, Pablo, 39
Pillow Talks, 37
Pilobolus, 19, 77
pliés, 89
Pollack, Jackson, 59

Post-Modern dance,
    65–66, 70, 79
Presidential Medals of
    Freedom, 67
Primary Accumulation
    (Brown), 65
Primus, Pearl, 56
Pulitzer Prizes, 52
Puremovement, 81
Push Comes to Shove
    (Tharp), 75–76
Pushkin, Aleksandr, 75

R

Radha (St. Denis), 25,
    30, 32
ragtime, 75
Rainer, Yvonne, 63
Rauschenberg, Robert, 60,
    62, 64
Re-Moves (Tharp), 72
Revelations (Ailey), 19, 67
Revolt (Graham), 43
Riverdance, 82
Robbins, Jerome, 75, 82–83
Roche, Pierre, 17
Rodeo, 82
Rodin, 17, 21
Rome and Jewels (Harris),
    81–82
Roof Piece (Brown), 63
"the runs", 10–11
Russia, 23
Ruth St. Denis School of
    Dancing. *See* Denishawn
    School

S

satire, 47
Seven New Dances
    (Taylor), 62
The Shakers (Humphrey),
    45–47
Shawn, Ted. *See also*
    Denishawn; Jacob's
    Pillow

as choreographer,
    34–37
death of, 38
Denishawn school
    and, 30
Graham and, 41
St. Denis and, 25, 27
Weidman and, 47
Shawn and His Men
    Dancers, 36–37, 38, 48
Shearer, Sybil, 90
Sherman, Jane, 28
Sikkema Jenkins & Co.,
    64
silence, 45–46
skirt dancing, 16
*So the Audience Does
    Not Know Whether I
    Have Stopped Dancing*
    (Brown), 64–65
Sonic Youth, 58
Spanish dance, 78
spirituality, 25
St. Denis, Ruth. *See also*
    Denishawn
    death of, 38
    fabric and, 19
    Fuller and, 17
    Graham and, 41–42
    overview of, 23–26
    as precursor to modern
        dance, 14
    Shawn and, 27, 35
stage dancing, 16
stock market crash, 40
Stravinsky, Igor, 39

T

Tamiris, Helen, 48,
    54–55
tap, 91
Taylor, Paul, 60–62, 66,
    69–70, 72
technology, 19
The Ten Commandments,
    34

tendu, 91
tennis, 69–70
Tharp, Twyla, 63, 65,
    70–76, 79
The Thief of Baghdad,
    34
Three Gopi Maidens
    (Graham), 42
As Time Goes By (Tharp),
    73
Toilers of the Soil
    (Denishawn), 33
Tony Awards, 55
Touch and Go, 55
Toulouse-Lautrec, Henri,
    17
Trend, 56
turnout, 89

U

University of California
    at Berkeley, 32–33

V

vaudeville, 31–32, 33,
    34–35
vernacular moves, 81
Vietnam War, 62, 72

W

Wade in the Waters, 19
Walking on the Wall
    (Brown), 65
Walks and Digressions
    (Gordon), 63
"Waltz of the Snowflakes",
    79
Webern, Anton von, 69
Weidman, Charles.
    See also Humphrey-
    Weidman Group
    Bennington College
        and, 50
    Dance Repertory
        Theater and, 48
    death of, 54

Denishawn and, 31, 36, 38

overview of, 47–48

West Side Story, 83

Wigman, Mary, 50, 60

Wilson, Sallie, 69

Works Project Administration, 55

World War I, 34

World War II, 37

Worth's Family Theater and Museum, 32

X

Xochitl, 35

Y

Yeats, William Butler, 17

Yesenin, Sergey, 23

Z

Zaide, 65

Ziegfeld Follies, 35

ABOUT THE AUTHOR AND CONSULTING EDITOR

Author **Janet Anderson** is a dance critic at Philadelphia's City Paper and was previously dance critic at the *Philadelphia Daily News*. She has written about dance for the *Philadelphia Inquirer*, *Seven Arts Magazine*, and PBS's show *Applause*. Prior to moving to Philadelphia, she was dance reviewer for the *Los Angeles Herald Examiner*, *Santa Monica Evening Outlook* and *Long Beach Press-Telegram*. She conducted and wrote Pew Charitable Trust's study on improving the quantity and quality of arts journalism. Ms. Anderson has an M.A. degree from University of North Carolina at Chapel Hill. Her Ph.D. is in process at the University of Texas Austin. Ms. Anderson's art/dance history dissertation is on Degas and his ballet images. She spent a year as special assistant to the chairman of the National Endowment for the Arts.

Consulting editor **Elizabeth A. Hanley** is associate professor emerita of Kinesiology at the Pennsylvania State University. She holds a BS in physical education from the University of Maryland and an MS in physical education from Penn State, where she taught such courses as modern dance, figure skating, international folk dance, square and contra dance, and ballroom dance. She is the founder and former director of the Penn State International Dance Ensemble and has served as the coordinator of the dance workshop at the International Olympic Academy, in Olympia, Greece.